TROUT WATERS

Other Publications

William O. Foye is editor of and contributor to *Principles of Medicinal Chemistry*, published by Lea & Febiger and available in three editions and five translations. The author is editor of *Cancer Chemotherapeutic Agents*, scheduled for publication in 1992 by the American Chemical Society. He is author of *A History of District One, National Association of Boards of Pharmacy—American Association of Colleges of Pharmacy*, Parts I and II. He has written approximately 150 research articles and reviews in the areas of organic, medicinal, and biological chemistry. He is contributor to

- *The Bulletin*, Massachusetts College of Pharmacy
- *Centerscope*, Boston University Medical Center
- *The Nucleus*, Northeastern Section of the American Chemical Society
- *The Herbarist*, The Herb Society of America
- *The Kirk-Othmer Encyclopedia of Chemical Technology*, published by John Wiley & Sons

Reminiscences with
a description of the
upper Quabbin Valley

TROUT WATERS

By
William O. Foye

Barbara Ellis

HALEY'S
Athol, Massachusetts

Library of Congress Catalogue Number: 91-065821
International Standard Book Number (ISBN): 0-9626308-1-0

Manufactured in the United States of America.
First Edition. First Printing. April 1992.

Book design by Mary Pat Spaulding and Marcia Gagliardi.
Cover painting ©1992 by Barbara Ellis.
Photographs since Quabbin flooding by Ellen Siddons.
Photographs before Quabbin flooding courtesy of J. R. Greene.
Maps drawn by Mary Pat Spaulding.
Text edited by Marcia Gagliardi.
Editorial consultation provided by Barbara Ellis, J. R. Greene,
  and James E. Herbert.
Copy read by Beverly Tarolli. Proof read by Arthur Tarolli.
Permission requested to reprint the poem on Page 84,
  originally published in *Muriel Foster's Fishing Diary*.
Text set on Apple Macintosh in Adobe Melior and Adobe Kabel.
Page layout in Aldus Pagemaker 4.01.
Printed by Adams Printing.

Haley's
P. O. Box 248
Athol, Massachusetts 01331

To my father and mother,
Owen H. Foye and Mildred R. Walton Foye

The author as a child with his parents

Remembrances

I grew up in a happy household with my father, mother, and Grandmother Foye. I do not recall ever hearing a quarrel. Rarely a harsh word passed among them, perhaps due to the strong personality of my father with his definite and clearly expressed views. He made the decisions, and they were seldom if ever questioned. Nevertheless, in such an apparently autocratic atmosphere, no attempt was made to influence me in the direction my life was to take. Incorrect or naughty behavior, however, was quickly dealt with.

All members of the family were avid readers. There was a sizable library of books collected by my grandparents and, although a significant part of it was represented in popular novels of their era—the 1890s and early 1900s—there were also a fair number of good United States and world history books. My father was particularly attracted to history. During the Depression of the Thirties when he was not too busy, he went through Edward Gibbon's *History of the Decline and Fall of the Roman Empire* and an almost as lengthy history of England. My mother and grandmother, before her eyesight became a problem, preferred more contemporary novels and biography. A scholarly aspect shared by my father and grandfather was the keeping of records. While none of my grandfather's records survived, my father's fishing journals present a good picture of trout populations in the area during the Twenties.

The family also enjoyed the company of guests of similar lively personalities. There were frequent visitors. Sometimes parties ran a bit too late into the night for our neighbors' tastes, and occasionally they reminded us of it. My father also woke them up quite early in the morning as he cranked up a particularly noisy car when he left for hunting or fishing. No one really complained, however. I believe our neighbors, generally of more sober dispositions, were fascinated by the good times and conviviality that were all too evident. There was also much humor and good feeling in the house whether during the prosperity of the Twenties or the straitened circumstances of the Thirties.

An aspect of our family life that was unusual for my boyhood friends was the almost constant presence of music. Both my mother and grandmother played the piano. My grandmother had also been the organist for her church, and my mother had played the piano in a movie theater in Gardner in concert with silent films. My father sang much of the time, both at home and while fishing. I still recall the words to popular songs of the Twenties and before. Like most young people, I found the early songs of the century quite amusing. My father's brother Arthur had an impressive voice and was a singer in some New York musicals in the Teens. It would seem natural that I would want to sing or play a musical instrument, but no amount of cajoling by my family convinced me to take piano lessons, and I was much too shy for solo singing. Early exposure did result in a lifelong appreciation of good music, but for that played by others than myself. The attraction of the woods and streams was of a more fatal nature, arousing a stronger desire to mingle with the forest trees and plants and to engage in active pursuits.

My mother had hoped that I might attend West Point. Colonel Ralph Drury, a family friend and retired Army officer, said he would assist my entrance if necessary. Fortunately, I did not meet one of the requirements for admission, 20:20 vision. The condition of my eyesight probably resulted from reading in bed to late hours with poor light. If I had studied at West

Point, I would most likely have been an early casualty in World War II. West Pointers who graduated in the beginning war years suffered a high casualty rate. A college friend of mine who transferred to West Point in 1941 was killed six months after going through a greatly accelerated training schedule.

My parents Owen and Mildred Foye were each quite handsome in appearance and attracted attention in any crowd. My father might be described as possessing an overpowering charm. He would find the more subdued and low key approach of many people today dull and deficient in feeling. He therefore formed friendships with people of similar lively personalities. Whenever there were gatherings of his friends in our house, whether they swapped tales of hunting and fishing or discussed other topics, I was fascinated and managed to listen in long after I was sent to bed.

My father was a man whose abilities were evidently not challenged by running the jewelry business my grandmother inherited at my grandfather's early death from angina. She brought her sons Owen and Arthur back to Athol to manage it: my father was then a student at Worcester Polytechnic Institute, and his brother was on the stage in New York or on tour. They both returned, and both gave up abilities that would likely have led to success in their chosen fields—chemistry for Owen, the stage for Arthur. Perhaps my father spent so much time in sporting activities, mainly fishing, hunting, and shooting, because he didn't find fulfillment in his business. The store was sold at auction in 1929 when my father foresaw the coming Depression and decided the business would not support two families. He acquired a considerable reputation as a sportsman, and when he died in 1957 while salmon fishing, the *Athol Daily News* carried the headline "Athol Sportsman Dies in Nova Scotia."

As I grew up in a small town, the woods and streams were within walking distance, and my sympathies and interests were directed early in life toward the wilds. Although I have worked in the city for many years, my lifelong interest—or more accurately, love—continues for the central Massachusetts wilderness. I believe I owe much to my parents, not only for instilling the more usual attributes of honesty, self-reliance, strong family relationships, and respect for others, but also for encouraging a strong attachment to nature. For this, I feel most fortunate and forever grateful.

Contents

Illustrations

Photographs

Maps

Foreword

Ten years ago this month, towards the end of a long lecture tour in India, I was enjoying the sunset from the verandah of the Rajasthan State Hotel. Eventually a figure appeared in the gathering darkness; introductions were duly made, and mutual professional recognition was instantaneous. If memory serves correctly, our membership in the "Brotherhood of the Angle" had been established even before we adjourned to the bar. Thus are friendships born....

During the ensuing years, Bill and his wife Lila have enriched my life with their kindness and hospitality and, in the process, have rekindled my love affair with the Commonwealth of Massachusetts, which commenced when two newlyweds settled in Cambridge some twenty-five years ago. It took but a little time to realise that Bill's self-effacement and modest demeanour conceal a number of passions: his family, his science, good fellowship, fly fishing, and conservation of the natural habitat, to name but a few. Bill's love of literature, particularly poetry, and—to quote Izaak Walton yet again—"such mirth as does not make friends ashamed to look upon one another next morning" ensure a flow of arresting conversation and wit: his letters are read many times before filing to be reread and thereby illuminate the dark winter evenings.

It is a particular pleasure to write this Foreword because the idea for such a volume arose out of a particularly happy experience shared with Bill (who proved once again that true anglers are born, not made) on one of Scotland's finest salmon rivers, the Aberdeenshire Dee. Following discussion and correspondence during the last three years, the original concept and resultant text have metamorphosed and evolved to their present form. At this point, it must be said that if your bibliographical quest is solely for heroic details of record bags or intricate details of the techniques of fishing, it will not be satisfied between these covers. Instead, Bill has embarked upon a rarer and much more difficult task: namely, to produce an integrated and entertaining account of people and events of a particular community encompassed by the clear and fast running streams of the Swift River watershed of western Massachusetts. He is uniquely qualified to do so: his antecedents were among the early English settlers of Massachusetts, and the first Foye was a Huguenot. The Foyes came via Britain to Boston and settled in Maine in the late 1600s. His branch of the Foye family has lived in Athol, Massachusetts, over 100 years. Bill's scientific distinction has afforded him considerable freedom of choice concerning where he would work and live. At a relatively early stage in his career, he elected to return to the state of his birth. There he has developed his science, acquired international recognition as an author, and taken appropriate steps to ensure that at least some of the streams and woods he loves so much will be preserved in their natural state. All this has been accomplished in that distinctive New England style, reflected perhaps in the laconic statement of Beatrix Potter's sartorially elegant frog, Jeremy Fisher: "I know a good place," he said, "for minnows. Fat minnows." Over the years, Bill has acquired a deep and abiding knowledge of the areas he describes, and his talents for observation and recording ensure accuracy of the text. His accomplished prose and sense of humour are a constant delight, and his affection for his subject illuminates the pages throughout.

It has been a privilege for me to explore, with Bill's guidance, the streams and woods so vividly described herein. I have admired his artistry with a small fly rod on the overgrown brooks and, like him, have found a profound sense of peace and harmony in these beautiful surroundings. It has been a pleasure to meet some of the people of the area, and I am confident that—whether you know the places concerned or do not, whether you fish or do not—you will feel this same sense of pleasure shared and enhanced through the pages of *Trout Waters.*

John M. Midgley
Glasgow, Scotland
December, 1991

The trout fly depicted on the cover is called "The Professor." The fly has a yellow body with gold ribbing, a brown hackle, a light colored, brown speckled wing, and a red tail. "The Professor" is fished wet—that is, under the surface as distinct from a dry fly intended to float on the surface.

Throughout the following chapters, I have elected to use present tense when referring to features of the Swift River Valley that have not been flooded by Quabbin Reservoir and therefore may still be visited. I have chosen to use past tense when referring to remembered places that are now flooded by Quabbin.

The references *Swift River Valley* or the *Valley* pertain to waters and surrounding land both before and since creation of Quabbin. *Quabbin Valley* refers to waters and surrounding land in the same area only since creation of the reservoir.

—William O. Foye

Bearsden Falls, Middle Branch of Swift River

The Magic Of A Trout Stream

THE RUSH OF WATERS. AMONG MY EARLIEST RECOLLECTIONS are the sounds of trout streams in central New England. The roar of streams was usually heard before they came into view, and when I was four or five, the surge of streams was fascinating, filling me with foreboding. No less exciting today, their sounds invoke anticipation and a sense of the primeval: the musical flow of rivulets, the shrill rushing of larger brooks, the dull roar of larger streams, the softer whisper of slow moving waters. Like the forested hills where they originate, each suggests a permanence dating at least to the last Ice Age. They bring excitement and feeling of life in earlier time, of the melting of glaciers and the return of forests. The magical sounds of streams do as much to transport the awed listener out of the present as do any of the other natural things we regard as permanent.

The branches and feeder streams of Swift River in central Massachusetts have all the variety of rushing, roaring, and whispering waters, along with a marvelous wealth of forests and vegetation that encloses them. My father fished much of this water, some now disappeared under Quabbin Reservoir. I was a child before the valleys were flooded, and I was exposed to their magical streams at an early age. Those lost waters were of exceptional beauty, and I remember them quite clearly. Their purity and breeding conditions produced a very sizable population of native brook trout.

Since I can recall many sections of the streams and have never seen descriptions of them in print, I am recording what I remember of them: pools and rapids, slow deep stretches, dark holes under logs and banks. Mystery and beauty surrounded the streams in overhanging boughs, towering pines, delicate curls of ferns, and heavy foliage of hardwoods. The magic was as much imprinted on my consciousness as the flow and music of the water. From such early memories—and a later realization of their importance as an aspect of permanence and sustenance—their elements of beauty and magic may have given my thoughts a direction as imperative as that of the streams themselves.

A trout stream is a marvelous creation of nature. It depends on a variety of well-balanced conditions including purity and temperature of water as well as bedrock of ridges from which the waters flow. Amount and purity of rainfall, intrusions of people and their domestic animals, weather, and the silvical characteristics of the watershed affect the ability of a stream to support a population of trout. Proximity of roads and dwellings may also be considered important—and usually detrimental.

I should add that people have yet to create a trout stream. Ponds, however, can be built and stocked with trout to allow fishing. Attempts to "create" a stream in which trout can survive and reproduce have been dismal failures. Aspects that go to "make" a trout stream worthy of the name, therefore, deserve recognition.

In the attempt to describe what "makes" a trout stream, however, I have included not only the appearance of the stream and the type of forest and plant life through which it flows, but also a sense of human associations that are part of a fisherman's lore. The presence of millponds, built by early settlers of the region, was an important aspect of the life of the stream. They frequently replaced the role of the former beaver ponds, often in the same locations. Ponds, whether for use of beavers or a commercial mill, provided trout with deep enough water for their survival during periods of low water. It is quite fortunate that the reintroduction of beavers in this region in the mid-1940s came very soon after the washout of many millponds in the floods of 1936 and 1938. Ponds then became again more or less permanent features of the streams.

All of these aspects, then, make a trout stream. Such characteristics of branches and tributaries of Swift River that have disappeared are found only in the recollections of individual fishermen and have not been generally recorded. Books and articles written by or for trout fishermen are usually concerned with techniques for catching trout or with amusing, exceptional, or heartwarming fishing episodes. Sometimes they are about the life and habits of trout or salmon inhabiting the streams. In general, descriptions of streams and their surroundings are not offered beyond a few sentences. I believe, however, that these aspects are important to fishermen and to those who traverse the banks in search of natural beauty.

Many streams of the Swift River watershed and their surrounding woods are still in existence and in a good state of preservation. Many others have disappeared, particularly the waters of the West Branch, which was most rich in both beauty and trout. Flooding Swift River's branches to make Quabbin Reservoir created a nature preserve and is of undoubted value as a water supply for today's urban industrial life, but the act also destroyed or forever altered beautiful habitats. To people to whom such things as a trout stream and their associations are of importance, I particularly wish to leave a record of waters flooded by Quabbin Reservoir. It is the combination and blending of all aspects of trout waters that led to my lifelong love affair with them, particularly those streams that make up the three branches of Swift River.

I have also attempted to give a brief view of our fathers' and grandfathers' methods of trout fishing. Before the days of the automobile, when much of the fishing was done in tributaries flowing through open fields, the long cane pole was used. Worms were the most common bait, and large numbers of rather small trout were caught. In fact, in the late 1800s and early 1900s, trout populations in this area were essentially those found under wilderness conditions. High populations left trout size relatively small, resulting in an average of five to eight inches. Only a few reached twelve inches or larger. Some of the larger streams could be fished successfully only with the much longer cast of the fly rod, and larger trout were found. It should be mentioned that trout scare very easily, and if trout see the fishermen, they dash for cover and cannot be caught. Bait fishermen fished these waters only in locations more favorable for their methods, or at night. Trout stocking by state and local fish and game clubs eventually supplied larger trout, but even the early years of stocking added trout of only six inches or less to the streams. Much trout fishing enjoyed today depends on stocking larger fish, but most are caught in the same year they are put into the stream. The native brook trout population has survived increased fishing pressure today, and many very small brooks fished by our grandfathers are now fished very little or not at all.

Providing water power for grist mills and sawmills, the three branches of the Swift River and their tributaries were also of great value to eighteenth and nineteenth century farming communities along their banks. At a time when close to two-thirds of the area was cleared for farm land (the greatest extent of cultivation is considered to be about 1835), the streams suffered very little change with the exception of the creation of millponds. Most such millponds are still traceable today, with their visible stone foundations or channels cut through banks to provide water from upstream. As a matter of historical interest, I have included sites of dams and millponds. Sometimes, such structures made by our ancestors are found on very small streams or in areas completely uninhabited today or some distance from a travelled road. Many stone foundations of mills are in a good state of preservation. Some mill foundations have suffered from vandals who pushed the stones into brooks to create dams that usually do not hold water. Our ancestors were much more successful at building dams by fitting stones together without benefit of cement, and their structures were so well made that, for the most part, they didn't leak.

The previous civilization of American Indians probably used the streams and the natural lakes left by glaciers mainly for fishing and transportation. The only traces of their habitation and use of the waters are the names still remaining of their villages and of some of the waters themselves. Quabbin and Neeseponsett are two notable examples. Although our present society has been the most destructive of the landscape and waterways, it is fortunate the remaining tributaries of the upper Swift River watershed are being kept in as wild a state as possible. Essentially wilderness waters, they may provide inspiration and beauty for those who require it. In the words of Aldo Leopold, "There are some who can live without wild things, and some who cannot." Thoreau was even more emphatic in stating our spiritual dependence on nature and its restorative effects. We can be thankful that this remnant of wilderness exists in an area so productive of forest growth and cold, rushing water. Trout can still make their spring migration up the brooks to feed and their fall migration to spawn. Although less visible than migrating hawks and waterfowl, trout can provide as great an excitement if the fisherman or nature lover is lucky enough to witness their migration. The ability of trout to survive in this or any watershed is very closely related to our own survival, since we are both dependent on the same water. The presence of trout in the cold, rushing waters of the Swift River, then, may be taken as symbolic of survival.

Because of my exposure at the earliest age to the beauty of the forests and streams of central New England, I have dedicated this book to my parents. By the time I was four or five, I had become acquainted with the pine and hemlock groves on the slopes leading to the rushing streams or boggy meadows below. I probably had a vague consciousness by the same age of the many moods of nature in the unsettled New England climate. At first, I sat in the car with my mother who read while waiting for my father to finish fishing his stretch of stream. When I was six or seven, I followed my father down those streams where the walking was safe. It was often a frustrating experience because of nearly impassable thickets or wide backwaters. It was frequently necessary to cross the stream, but that was always a welcome part of the trip. Clinging to my father's back while he carefully maneuvered his way across the current seemed to provide feelings of certainty and warmth. If I were left behind, surrounded by seemingly immense ferns and undergrowth where snakes or other wildlife might be lurking, it often led to tears. Once, when a turtle blocked my passage on a sand bar, my bawling caused it to put its head back in its shell and crawl into the water. Despite such frightening possibilities of the streams and their mysterious surroundings, I grew up with a strong attachment to the waters and the nearby overcrowding forests.

Other scenic aspects of the Swift River watershed for which I have a lasting recollection, a feeling of kinship, and even a sense of belonging are the remaining farms with their surrounding fields, stone walls, and sometimes rail fences—and always pine groves beyond. When I was a child, many farms were already being encroached upon by surrounding pines and birches. Today, seeing rural areas in such a state of uneasy equilibrium with invading trees rather fills me with nostalgia; the clearing of forests to provide new fields or pastures presents to me a much less pleasing view. With similar nostalgia, I also recall farm people who lived near the streams. I remember particularly their friendly but laconic demeanor. There were some farmhouses and backrooms of inns where home-brewed beer was available during the Prohibition years. My favorite of these establishments probably was the bar at the Greenwich Inn, run by Andy Merritt, where I was allowed to perch on the bar and sample the foam.

As for the veracity of the anecdotes related, I have to rely on the integrity of those from whom I heard them—for whom I can vouch—and of those who relayed them to my sources. For those secondary sources, some of whom I knew as a child, I must believe, with Emerson and Thoreau, in the integrity of the New England countryman. In this respect, I can quote from an ancestor, whose family resided at one time in Enfield: "I may not have added to the family fortune, but I kept the family name unsullied."

The fishing gear used by George H. "Harry" Foye about 1906, including a straw hat, worm can, grasshopper coop, canvas creel, and sixteen-foot cane pole

Owen Foye's fishing gear, used about 1917, including a catgut leader soaked to use, fly book for snelled flies, felt hat, wicker creel, and Meadow Brook eight-and-one-half-foot split-cane fly rod

Fishing gear used in 1991 by William O. Foye, including a six-and-one-half-foot Fenwick glass fly rod, fly-casting reel, and fly boxes

Fishing rods from three generations lined up for comparison

A shaded stretch of the East Branch

The Watershed

THE WATERSHED OF THE TRIBUTARIES OF SWIFT RIVER in west central Massachusetts above the former junction of its three branches in Enfield is an area of much diversity of stream types and surrounding forests. The forests are a meeting ground for northern hardwood and central forests of oak and pine. The area may not have the richness and variety of a tropical forest, but its luxuriance—and in places magnificence—of growth provide singular interest and astonishment not to be found in forests farther north. A few species of trees of a more southern prevalence are also found in an occasional Swift River Valley representative, such as the sycamore. Boggy areas left from retreating glaciers are remnants of northern boreal forests. Spruce and tamarack were most prevalent just after the ice melted; they now provide the area with pockets of a more arctic and solitary aspect.

Now dominating the landscape, however, is the Eastern white pine. In every direction, it creates a ragged and feathery view on the horizon of the tops and upper branches of these rather primitive trees. Whether the view is of sunrise or sunset, of brilliant sun-flooded day or of drooping rain, Eastern white pine tops are an awe inspiring part of the scene. I am always thrilled by the reminder of home when I catch a view of pines against the sky in other areas of the country or world. Pines also play a role in the diversity of growth of flowering plants on the forest floor. Their spreading branches provide shelter for a variety of plant species while allowing enough sunlight through to support a wealth of plant life. In a pine grove or mixed pine/hardwood grove, the ground is carpeted with a variety of plants that flower throughout the spring and summer. The same function of protection and partial sunlight also allows a diverse growth of fungi of various and striking colors under conditions of the right temperature and moisture. Moisture trapped in the groves gives rise to sometimes heavy fogs that may curl up through pine tops in startling shapes or blanket the area in a luminous darkness. In winter, similar effects are especially impressive. Small vapor clouds escape through the trees and waft like scuds of froth on a seashore. After snowstorms, snow clouds blown from pine boughs resemble wisps of fog that escape at warmer times. Against a blue sky after snow, they give the watershed aspects of beauty recalling the primitive, untouched state of nature on this continent before Europeans invaded.

Forests sheltering the various streams of the watershed have an extensive intrusion of the Eastern hemlock with its lacy and upturned branches that give the area an Oriental quality. The hemlock is a rare tree in much of North America. Only four species of this Asiatic-appearing tree are found on this continent; many more are found in the Orient. With its fine needles and the graceful upturn of its lower branches, it resembles the upturned ridgepoles, gates, and roofs of Oriental pagodas and buildings. It may be buildings were patterned after the hemlock when they were first designed in China. In the mixed hardwood and evergreen forests of central New England, however, the Eastern hemlock is a common tree with dense groves in the lower swampy regions of the watershed or scattered soaring individuals on higher elevations. The supple, drooping tops of hemlocks bend under and rarely break from wet snows and ice storms. Plentiful rainfall in the watershed makes this tree well suited to growing conditions. The lacy, Oriental aspect of young hemlocks pushing their way up through the solemn trunks of mature trees softens the often grim aspect of dense groves. To Emily Dickinson, the hemlock was symbolic of wilderness "and satisfies an awe." To me, the hemlock provides both utilitarian value in trapping moisture in the groves and beauty not found with other, but no less majestic, trees.

Under groves dominated by hemlock, much less plant life makes a footing. Only species most tolerant of shade are found. In groves primarily of hemlock with great age, almost no plant life is found on the floor. In general in this region, however, other climax hardwoods and white pines are present, so enough sunlight is admitted for some plant species to survive. Bunchberry, clintonia, and trillium are often found in the groves, and the edges are often lined with hobblebush or mountain laurel. Hemlock groves with their restrictive admission of sunlight often "light up" when mists or sparse fogs invade the woods. They become almost brilliant after fresh snow has left their boughs covered or frost has encased them with hoar.

No such aspects of beauty, however, can be found in the Scotch pine groves planted in old fields within the Quabbin reservation. In groves of Scotch pine, not native to the area, no plant growth survives on the forest floor, and there are no lower branches to hold snow or ice. Ice storms often mow them down, groves at a time, because they lack the suppleness of either white pine or hemlock. The extent of their growth over a fifty year period has been disappointing and far less than that of the native white pine, which would have seeded in naturally. Since the Scotch pines have not grown large enough to constitute timber that can be harvested, they are now being cleared out and salvaged for wood chips.

The upper Swift River watershed has a catchment area of about one hundred eighty-six square miles. It is very hilly country with long ridges running from north to south and a number of pyramid shaped hills jutting abruptly from the valleys. Many southern ends of ridges as well as valley pyramids have the sharp, truncated feature characteristic of a glaciated area. They provide contrast to the rolling landscape farther east. Valleys in this area are on the average about five hundred feet above sea level, and the ridge tops are usually six or seven hundred feet higher. Hillsides are usually quite steep and in places difficult to climb. Many are obstructed with huge boulders, often given an aspect of antiquity by encrustations of rock lettuce and overhanging clusters of polypody. Valleys are further interrupted by eskers of sand left by the glaciers. They usually support good growths of pine. The flat plain formerly in the Middle Branch valley, then, was a surprising aspect. It stretched approximately from Thompson Pond, northeast of Millington, to Enfield on the south, and from the Prescott ridge to hills bordering branches of Fever Brook to the east.

The hilly country of central Massachusetts with its rather narrow valleys was the last area of the present Commonwealth east of the Connecticut River valley to be settled by English colonists. Settlers moved in both from the eastern end of the colony and from the Connecticut valley mainly in the 1730s. Townships were incorporated roughly twenty years later: New Salem in 1753, Petersham in 1754, Greenwich in 1754, Shutesbury in 1761. Other watershed towns resulted when parishes and original townships separated or one or more areas combined. Dana was incorporated in 1801, formed from parts of Petersham, Greenwich, and Hardwick. Enfield separated from Greenwich and, with a section of Belchertown, was incorporated as a town in 1816. Prescott, first settled in the 1740s, was formed from the East Parish of Pelham and a section of southern New Salem. It became a town in 1822.

Relative lateness in settling the watershed may have been due to a greater presence of Indians than in other colonial settings. Or, more likely, hilly and exceptionally rocky terrain made establishing farms a backbreaking enterprise. There was a settled community of Indians in Pequoig, now Athol, where fertile fields existed for planting corn. It lies just north of the Quabbin watershed. Athol was first inhabited by English settlers in 1735, and the fact that three forts were built in the eastern, central, and western sections of town indicates that

Indians, not too pleased at being displaced, still hunted and roamed the area. I have no knowledge of permanent Indian settlements in the three valleys of the Swift River, but one apparently existed in the flat plain of Greenwich. A Nipmuc Indian chief named Nini-Quabbin or Nani-Quabbin had once lived in that area. Other Indian names in the watershed which have survived are Pottapaug Pond on the East Branch and Neeseponset Pond on the Middle Branch. The relative scarcity of Indian names surviving in the Swift River area may be due to the paucity of fixed Indian settlements. However, there was also a tendency of English settlers to commemorate the names of towns of origin in England, like Petersham and Greenwich; towns of origin in eastern Massachusetts, like Salem; names of dukes on whose land they had lived in Scotland, like Athol. More detailed information concerning establishment of Swift River Valley towns may be found in local histories, or in a concise summary in J. R. Greene's *An Atlas of the Quabbin Valley, Past and Present* published in 1975 by The Transcript Press in Athol.

    The Indian inhabitants of the region had been mostly driven out by the Indian Wars of the late 1600s or had died from contracting white settlers' diseases. Few Indian families remained to witness the cutting of the forests and removal of rocks to form the stone wall boundaries of settlers' farms. The presence of forts in the early settlements did not indicate that people of European origin co-existed with Indians, as was the case further east in Natick. One of the last records of a surviving Indian in this region concerns an old man living at the junction of the two branches of Tully Brook in Orange until his death in 1832.

    Europeans brought a different style of living to the Valley, and the establishment of colonial farms in the hills was an arduous undertaking. After cutting sizable forest areas for fields, farmers removed tons of rocks to permit plowing that was accomplished through manual labor and assisted by oxen pulling stoneboats. Stone walls were well crafted, and many remain today with little alteration from frost heaves or instability. Labor was not required to such an extent in more hospitable areas to the east or west. The hard land must have led to relatively early abandonment of many hill farms as soon as the Midwest was opened for settlement in the first half of the nineteenth century. By the 1890s and the first decade of the 1900s, white pine groves that had sprung up in abandoned fields of deserted farms were being clear cut for lumber. Now, a hundred years later, clear-cut areas have often reverted to the mixed forest present before the land was cleared. Present forestry practices in the area are mainly selective for mature or less suitable specimens of trees. It is fortunate that a relatively sizable region of what was formerly called the best pine belt in central New England has survived and is now closer to its pre-colonial type of mixed growth. With increased demands for housing, however, and some reestablishment of small farms, some forest restoration is being lost.

The difficulty and hard labor of maintaining farms in the Swift River Valley and other regions of western Massachusetts must also have been a factor in the eruption of Daniel Shays' Rebellion in 1786 and 1787. The Rebellion was a significant factor leading to abandonment of the Articles of Confederation and adoption of the United States Constitution. Perhaps a more independent spirit had developed in the hills, or farmers were "up against it" to a greater degree than elsewhere in the state. In any case, the imposition of new taxes by the fledgling pre-Constitutional Commonwealth led to an attempt in 1787 by the farmers of the region to seize Springfield Armory. Daniel Shays of Pelham headed the contingent. Troops of state militia quickly put down the uprising, however, and the rebellious farmers disappeared back into their hills. They wore sprigs of hemlock in their hats, perhaps an indication of regard for their wild surroundings.

As the 1800s progressed, abandoned watershed farms quickly reverted to forest in an environment of favorable rainfall and quick growth of resident species. Very little industry ever became established in Swift River valleys, and the area had become a sparsely populated, mainly forested region by the early 1900s. Unfortunately, politicians and engineers of the Boston area considered the small population of the area a major factor in selecting Swift River as a site for the Quabbin Reservoir to supply the Boston area which grew short of water by the Twenties. A plan for a reservoir was passed by the state legislature in 1927, with little fanfare and surprisingly little objection by the people and their representatives from western Massachusetts. There would, no doubt, be much more objection raised today, but the prevailing attitude of the time was, "You can't get in the way of progress." The process of removing remaining inhabitants of the region, generally referred to as "the Valley," took place in the Thirties. On April 28, 1938, the four towns of Dana, Enfield, Greenwich, and Prescott legally ceased to exist. Many of the Valley residents settled in surrounding towns. To their lasting credit, they formed the Swift River Valley Historical Society to preserve pictorial records of towns, villages, and families of the area. Artifacts, paintings, and memorabilia housed at their museum in North New Salem present a picture of rural life in the 1800s hardly touched by industrial and urban problems.

A West Branch beaver pond

Hemlock mirrored in another West Branch beaver pond

Remains of a West Branch beaver dam

The West Branch

The West Branch Above Cooleyville

WEST BRANCH WATERS ORIGINATE IN THE SWAMPS AND BOGS of Wendell, amid ancient hemlock groves and mixed pine and hardwood forests that today retain much of their former wildness. The wet and spongy woods support a lavish undergrowth of plants, at least in the pine and hardwood stands. Skunk cabbage, trout lily, clintonia, trillium (white and painted), star flower, jack-in-the-pulpit, partridgeberry, wild sarsaparilla, false hellebore, bunchberry, various species of lycopodium, hobblebush, and ferns are commonly found in these woods. There are also variously colored fungi that spring up after summer showers. Ferns are everywhere, and in years with wet spring seasons, the great osmundas stand shoulder high. Along the streams are found royal fern in addition to cinnamon, interrupted, and sensitive ferns. In drier locations are evergreen wood fern, Christmas fern, and polypody. The maidenhair fern has been shaded out of many locations but can still be found. Vines of river grape are also prevalent along this and other streams of the area.

Two branches of the upper West Branch come together at a place once called New Boston. The foundations of a former mill and dam along with stoned-in water diversions have survived the depredations of weather, high water, and people. Such remains are found on most Swift River branches and tributaries. The easterly branch has a relatively large beaver pond of more than ten acres, as well as a number of other beaver ponds. The westerly branch is mainly a rocky, cascading stream racing its way in wild fashion most of the distance to Cooleyville, the junction of the three streams that constitute the main body of the West Branch. Although much of the stream consists of rather shallow pools and pockets, there are occasional pools of good depth. Some long runs of sufficient depth once held good trout.

A pool below the New Boston area is one of my particular favorites. It is easily viewed from the road, a dirt road just wide enough for two cars to pass, and I seldom fail to stop for a view, or to fish. The pool is probably eighty to ninety yards long with a shelving ledge on one bank and a light gravel bottom. The forest is mature, with very little undergrowth, mostly of hobblebush, and the tall trunks of hemlock, birch, maple, oak, ash, and pine stand distinct, even in twilight. Although the pool is relatively shallow for most of its length, the lower end is much deeper, shaded by overarching hemlocks and hardwoods. The pool formerly held a good population of trout, and the deeper end often sheltered trout of a pound or so. Because of the clarity of the water and lack of depth, fine tackle was required to catch them. I have spent many pleasant evenings in the attempt.

With the exception of about the last mile above Cooleyville, few trout stayed in this stretch during periods of low water. When formerly present in much greater numbers, they ran up this brook when high water resulted from the two- or three-day rains of the region. One such spate occurred on the last day of July in 1916, then the final day of legal trout fishing for the season. Wally Powers, Russell Furbush, and my father were in Cooleyville on that date and had no difficulty in "filling their baskets" from the swarm of trout that went up the three brooks that come together in Cooleyville. They had a copious lunch composed of boiled lobster and raw clams, and my father related that Wally then had a difficult time walking uphill on the road going up the valley of the West Branch. Wally had been raised in Cooleyville and was known for his inventiveness, both for mechanical innovations and for vocabulary. He caught one particularly good-sized trout weighing close to a pound in a pool near the road. In his humorous fashion, Wally stated the trout would never have gotten off the hook, since he had hooked him "in the appalachio." I trust his walk back to Cooleyville was more pleasurable.

Russell Furbush, from Westford, was at the time a detective working for the federal government in Athol. His particular duty was to keep an eye out for possible wartime saboteurs who might damage manufacturing plants, especially the tool factories there. He evidently saw no immediate danger of this kind, since he spent a good deal of time trout fishing during that and the following summer.

Although most of the West Branch above Cooleyville is rock bottomed and paved with cobbles, gravel deposits become evident in the last mile. Gravel may delineate the extent of a lake created during the retreat of the last glacier. The character of the stream changes noticeably during this stretch, and trout inhabit it throughout the summer and fall. The drop in elevation from the junction of the two branches at New Boston to the Cooleyville ponds is two hundred five feet over a distance of about two and a half miles.

The remains of another large stone dam are found about halfway between New Boston and Cooleyville. Just above Cooleyville, a channel for diverting water may be seen leading toward a millpond on the other, or easterly branch, but there is no sign of a stone dam at the site of diversion. The dam at this point must have been a wooden one, now rotted and washed away. A wooden dam existed up to the present time at the point where the two main branches of the stream joined at Cooleyville. The number of mills on these streams gives some indication of how many farms were in the region during the 1700s and 1800s. Today, the area is completely returned to forest, with the exception of a few houses in the Cooleyville area. Despite an increasing but still small invasion of residences along the roads to the north and west of these two main branches, the forest has been preserved. Shutesbury State Forest and the Metropolitan District Commission (MDC), which has the responsibility of preserving the watershed of the Quabbin Reservoir, have prevented further inroads.

Forests along the upper reaches of the West Branch are mainly of two types, hemlock groves and mixed pine and hardwood stands. Hemlock groves also include some hardwoods, such as maple, oak, and ash with the occasional beech as well as the ever present pine. The pine and hardwood forests include red and white maple; red, black, white, scarlet, and chestnut oak; black, white, and yellow birch; white ash, black cherry, white pine; an occasional pitch pine; and a scattering of smaller trees, such as hop hornbeams.

Blight-infected chestnut saplings are becoming ever more abundant in this region and appear to be growing to greater heights—thirty feet or more—before they succumb. Apparently, roots are unaffected by the blight-causing organism and are putting up vigorous shoots seventy years after the complete loss of mature trees of this species in New England. A fungus caused the blight, and by 1920, essentially all chestnut trees in New England had been killed. Blight spread throughout the eastern range of the tree, and living chestnuts are gone with the exception of a few isolated trees and a few recent plantings.

The forests are dominated by white pine, however, that rise above other trees and create a ragged but inspiring skyline. Northern red oak with its spreading crown and long, branchless trunk also gives an over-arching cathe-dral air to groves where it dominates. In early June, the woods are brightened by occasional bouquets of June pink, and they are positively festooned with the pink and white bloom of mountain laurel later in the month. In some higher elevations above Cooleyville struck by the hurricane of 1938, laurel became so thick as to be impenetrable, but laurel thickets are gradually being shaded out as the forest matures.

Canada Brook

THE EASTERLY OF THE TWO PRINCIPAL BRANCHES OF THE WEST BRANCH above Cooleyville was known as Canada Brook to residents of that area and to trout fishermen of the early part of the century. It has its origins in Wendell, with one upper fork starting less than a mile from the pond where the Middle Branch of Swift River starts. The two forks that constitute the main stream come together in a large, spongy bog formerly called Cranberry Meadow. The bog is now a beaver pond close to a third of a mile in length and has probably existed as such on and off for centuries. When no beavers were present, roughly from the late 1700s to the 1950s, or when beavers abandoned the pond, cranberry bushes grew among bog plants that sprang up when the pond subsided to the main channel and back waters of the stream. Below Cranberry Meadow, the stream flows over a rocky bed but appears markedly different from the upper reaches of the westerly branch. The rocks are darker in hue, and there are more large boulders in the stream bed. Sheer ledges slope gently or sometimes precipitously into the stream more often than in the upper West Branch. Beavers occasionally flood several slower stretches to create long still pools of appreciable depth.

Much of the forest along this branch is dominated by hemlock groves that give a more open aspect to the forest. Most plant life found on the westerly branch is also found along Canada Brook, although in much less profusion. In May, however, large white blooms of hobblebush peer out from the dense shade of hemlocks and maples. Some quite large white pines are present in good numbers, as well as some magnificent red oaks. Many of the majestic oaks, unfortunately, were killed by the gypsy moth infestation of 1979 to 1981, but a few remain to reseed whenever an opening occurs in the forest from wind or other tree death.

There are several stretches of stream where the brook descends quite rapidly with small but scenic falls. They are not precipitous but consist of series of cascades with the water tumbling over boulders or through well-worn sluices in the rocks. From Cranberry Meadow to Cooleyville, a distance of about three miles, the drop in elevation is three hundred thirty feet. Comparatively, the westerly branch from New Boston to Cooleyville drops two hundred five feet.

At Cooleyville, Canada Brook enters a formerly large millpond, with parts of the stone dam in good preservation. The pond is now a beaver pond, which

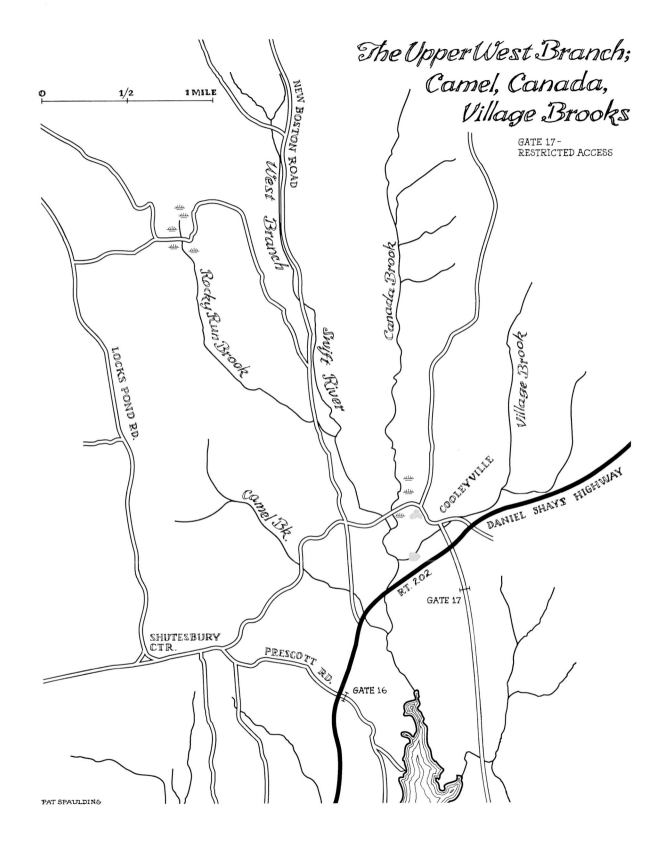

The Upper West Branch; Camel, Canada, Village Brooks

GATE 17 –
RESTRICTED ACCESS

0   1/2   1 MILE

NEW BOSTON ROAD

West Branch

Rocky Run Brook

Swift River

Canada Brook

Village Brook

LOCKS POND RD.

Camel Bk.

COOLEYVILLE

DANIEL SHAYS HIGHWAY

R.T. 202

GATE 17

SHUTESBURY CTR.

PRESCOTT RD.

GATE 16

PAT SPAULDING

it no doubt was before the millpond was created. The stone foundation of a mill is found a short distance below Cranberry Meadow. Another channel for water diversion may be seen about a mile above Cooleyville, but no evidence of dam or mill remains. From this point to the millpond at Cooleyville, the stream flows over a rocky channel more resembling the westerly branch, with fewer boulders or rock ledges found upstream.

On the ridge east of Canada Brook was a small settlement known as Macedonia. Its cellar holes are still visible, but now they support trees of mature size. Macedonia was the home of a family by the name of Juckett, and local legend describes the encounter of Old Man Juckett with federal agents during the Civil War. They had come to conscript his strapping teenaged son. Juckett is supposed to have taken a stand on a rock to state, "By the Great God Jehovah and the Constitution of the United States, you ain't gonna take him." As in most such encounters, Juckett was unsuccessful. Legend does not tell us the fate of the younger Juckett or whether he survived the war. If he did, he could not have maintained the farm in that rocky environment for too many years, since Macedonia was deserted by the early 1900s.

Much of Canada Brook flows through the quite mature Shutesbury State Forest. Very little undergrowth is found in hemlock groves along the brook, but the forest becomes more diversified going up the slopes on either side. With the reintroduction of beaver meadows and preservation of the forest, the area has a most wild and pristine appearance.

Village Brook

THE THIRD STREAM THAT JOINS THE EASTERLY AND WESTERLY BRANCHES of the West Branch at Cooleyville was known to those living nearby as Village Brook. Smaller than the other two arms of the West Branch, it originates about two miles east of its confluence with the West. In appearance, Village Brook is much different from the rest of the West Branch. Village Brook flows for the most part over a sandy, light-bottomed bed, with more water plants growing in the stream. Two forks join in the upper reaches to form a delightful little stream, and once again are found the remains of a stone dam, partially grown over. Periodically beavers convert it to a beaver dam, recreating the pond. Other beaver ponds exist occasionally in both Village Brook forks. There is no more than a mile of the beautiful little stream from the junction of its two branches at the old mill dam to the point where it joins the West Branch just below Cooleyville. The drop in elevation over this distance is about one hundred forty-five feet.

An attempt to build a trout pond in a small marshy area just off the course of the brook a short distance above the West Branch was made in the early Forties by Wally Powers, who grew up in Cooleyville in the last decade of the 1800s and the first decade of the 1900s. He placed a cement dam between marsh and brook and diverted some brook water into the dammed-up marsh. Wally stocked trout in the resulting pond, but they immediately left it. Swamp water was evidently not to their liking. Wally then put in screens at inlet and outlet, but the trout managed to get around them. Wally abandoned his attempt to establish a trout pond. Similar attempts in the Swift River area have met with similar failure. Two cement dams have been built on or just off Shattuck Brook: the brook cut a new channel around one dam, and the other fills with algae in the summer. However, beavers dammed Wally's pond in the late Seventies, and a trout population became established there. Apparently the slow flow of water through the leaky beaver dam provided the necessary oxygen, temperature, and aquatic insects for the trout's survival.

The fertile valley and hillsides along Village Brook support the growth of exceptionally tall pines, and there is more hardwood in the forests. The gypsy moth invasion of the early Eighties caused less destruction to the oaks here than along Canada Brook, probably because of their comparative youth. I understand that much of the area along this brook was cleared for fields and pasture by the early part of this century, and some old field pine stands are still evident.

Another stone dam that was never washed out is found on Village Brook in Cooleyville. The floods of 1936 and 1938 filled the pond with sand and mud. Today the channel through it is relatively deep compared with the one- to two-foot depth of the rest of the brook. The brook then races rapidly through what remains of the village of Cooleyville—ten or twelve houses, depending on where you put the boundaries. Although Village Brook and other streams supported mills and provided water power for the settlers of the 1700s and 1800s, such industry did not alter the streams to any extent. Millponds in many locations merely replaced what had been beaver ponds, providing the trout populations with gathering places during periods of low water, as had beaver ponds previously.

Brook trout populations of these streams must have been enormous, compared to those of today. Villagers would go trout fishing in a group when the brooks were high, according to Wally Powers, and large numbers of trout from downstream would congregate in the Cooleyville area. The fishermen collected their catch in a laundry tub and generally had it filled after fishing no more than a half mile from the village. Wally also told of days when he caught between thirty and forty fish, many of which were "short trout" of less than the six inch legal limit of the time. He loved to eat the small fish, claiming they had a better flavor than larger trout, and he ate them like sardines—bones and all.

Perhaps the major characteristic of all these streams is the clarity of the water. They are exceptionally clear and colorless, and the well used appellation of "gin-clear" certainly applies. Only after heavy downpours when the brooks go over their banks does the water become clouded with silt. Flooding usually lasts for very brief periods. The West Branch below New Boston has recently experienced some filling of its rock-bottomed pools with gravel, some from washouts of the gravel road just below the former easterly branch mill diversion. High water runoff flows down the road itself. No filling of pools was evident prior to the warming trend of the 1980s, when heavy winter rains washed away much gravel and other debris from the flood plain. Before the warming trend, winter precipitation had been primarily snow. Along most of the West Branch, however, are found numerous overflow channels that accommodate much of the high water. Along the West Branch in the spring can now be seen leaves and sticks lodged against trees and rocks two or three feet above the normal stream level. Previous floods must also have lodged debris high above stream level, but it was not as common on a yearly basis, in my recollection, as today.

The Cooleyville Ponds

The lower end of Canada Brook flows into a large marsh in Cooleyville. The upper marsh was the former site of a millpond, but beavers now restore it periodically. The millpond was known to fishermen as Zahn's Pond, probably from the name of the operator of the mill during the early 1900s. The remainder of the marsh below the road is also flooded by beavers, and this flowage has been inhabited more or less permanently by beavers since their return to the area in the early 1950s. It also provides good habitat for other pond dwelling wildlife, but apparently fishermen and others are too often present to encourage duck nesting. Ducks do use the ponds during the spring and fall migrations. Black and wood ducks are generally seen, with an occasional mallard or hooded merganser. The woodcock summers in the area, and an occasional grouse is now seen. During the early part of the century, with the return of the orchards and pastures to birch, alder, poplar, and young pine, the area around this marsh was prime grouse and woodcock cover. Today, a few ancient apple trees have survived in pine groves of considerable height. The cedar waxwing is also found here in numbers. The whippoorwill was also regularly heard on the slope to the east, but I have not heard one in this spot for the last few summers. Perhaps the forest has matured too much for whippoorwills. I also miss hearing the sound of the hermit thrush. Formerly, the plaintive, thrilling sound of hermit thrush could be heard in several exact locations north of the marsh in the spring and early summer until mid-July, but much less in recent years. Forests north of the marsh have been altered to a small extent by occasional selective logging, but enough mature groves survive to provide the shady habitat preferred by hermit thrush. We might conclude that the absence of the bird in this area is due more to the loss of its winter habitat, Central American tropical forests, than of summer habitat.

Following one logging operation just north of this area several years ago, and simultaneously one bordering Cranberry Meadow, a number of the resident hawks and owls moved into the relatively undisturbed forests in between. For a couple of summers after, the barred owl and several species of hawks were common in these woods. Now these mature forests, which would appear to support less animal life than the thinned forests to the north and south, have returned to their previous quiet state, where the hawk or owl is only occasionally detected. During the 1984 to 1985 period of high hawk and owl populations, I recall an evening on the upper Canada Brook when I was fly casting for trout and whistling a rather shrill tune. A hawk swooped rapidly to a perch directly overhead. I was amazed at the extreme accuracy with which the hawk had pinpointed the sound, apparently taken for a bird song. One flick of the rod, however, sent the hawk as rapidly out of there.

Besides the millpond on Canada Brook at Cooleyville, there was also a pond with a wooden dam at the junction of the two main branches of the West Branch. The dam served mainly to supply water through a diversion to a millpond off the main stream, where a sawmill operated until 1945 or 1946. Charley Frost was the last operator. The millpond was known as Lucius Lawless Pond, apparently after an early owner. At the junction of the two branches, the pond was referred to as Mother's Pond by Wally Powers, since his mother owned the land around it. The wooden dams of Mother's and Lawless ponds have now mostly disappeared, but during spates, Lawless Pond still holds some water. There are also the remains of a cement dam in a small swampy area east of the large beaver pond on the last stretch of Canada Brook below Shutesbury Road. It is obviously of much more recent origin, but its purpose remains a mystery.

When the sawmill was in operation on Lawless Pond, some sawdust got into the brook, and dead trout with their gills clogged could be found for some distance below the mill. Millponds provided a refuge for trout during periods of very high or low water, however. The same function was formerly provided by the beaver ponds, and is now, again. The millponds of Cooleyville held sizable numbers of trout throughout the spring, summer, fall, and perhaps the winter. I have seen trout in them up until the time the ice covered them in November.

These streams of the West Branch support primarily the brook trout, *Salvelinus fontinalis*. Brown and rainbow trout stocked in both the stream itself and the Quabbin Reservoir have been present at times but have not established a native population. The salmon stocked in the Quabbin now spawn in the West Branch, however, and salmon parr with an occasional smolt are now found in the West Branch both above and below Cooleyville, but in greater numbers below. Both the young salmon and trout appear to coexist in the same areas of the stream.

As for other species of fish that may be present, I know of only one instance when such was determined. One night in the 1920s, Wally Powers attempted to net the trout in Mother's Pond. He placed a net across the stream below the dam. He pulled a plug at the base of the sloping, wooden dam with the expectation that trout would swim downstream with the flow of water. No fish were found in the net. Wally and his companions then went upstream with flashlights looking for the fish and found them packed in the pool under and below the bridge on the West Branch. They saw not only trout, but horned pout, suckers, and pickerel as well. The dace, which is found in most of the waters of central Massachusetts, has not become established in West Branch waters, probably because of the size of the native trout population. One is found only occasionally today. Bluegills and sunfish are now present in the warmer water where the stream mingles with the water of the reservoir, however.

Wally Powers had a son Laurence whom I had never met. Laurence knew both my parents, however. Late one afternoon, more than twenty years after the Quabbin area was open to fishing, I had parked my car at a pullout beside the Daniel Shays Highway. With little daylight left, I was in a hurry to get to the stream to fish. Another car was parked there, and the driver got out, came over while I gathered my tackle, and obviously wanted to talk to me. I was impatient to get going, but something about the gentleman, his voice, and his manner of speaking had a vague familiarity, and I was polite enough to chat for a short while. As we talked, we were peering into one another's eyes with identical questioning intensity. Like me, he was evidently trying to recall where we might have met before. It was not until I had left and walked a short distance down the road to the stream that it became apparent who he must have been: Laurence Powers. The voice was very similar to Wally's, and his question of "Are there any trout left down there at all?" was exactly the way Wally would have put it. I described him to my mother when I returned home, and she thought the description fit Laurence quite well. It was a strange encounter; we each apparently recognized traits in the other that resembled those of the father. I have often wondered whether Laurence came to the right conclusion regarding my identity. I intended at the time to look him up in Springfield, where he lived, but I never did.

The West Branch Below Cooleyville

BELOW THE COOLEYVILLE PONDS, THE MAIN STREAM typically has a gravel bottom that is now and then sandy, indicating the extent of a glacial lake probably found on Swift River when the most recent glacier retreated. From Cooleyville downstream, the bottom is paved with the lemon-yellow stones that, with the sand, give the water its bright appearance. Bordering on the stream are woods of mixed pines, hardwoods, and hemlock that harbor a great profusion of wild flowers. More pitch pine with their wild, unkempt aspect once grew in the area but have been diminished in number by logging. The white puffs of the shad bush in early May were also more numerous earlier in the century when abandoned fields of the area were being taken over by birch, poplar, and pine.

In the region formerly known as Dickeyville about three miles below Cooleyville, elm trees became noticeable in the valley and, in company with immense white pines, created a most majestic forest. Some very ancient hemlocks were also found along the stream, and their stumps are evident during periods when the Quabbin Reservoir is low. The rate of fall of the stream is less than that above the ponds: from Cooleyville to the junction of branches at Enfield, a distance of about eleven and a half miles, the stream had a drop of about one hundred fifty feet. The force of the current, however, particularly during very high water, was such that it was difficult to wade in most stretches. So the stream justified its name, Swift River. In some instances, it has been impossible to wade the stream anywhere below the junction of the branches in Cooleyville.

Immediately below Cooleyville, the stream flows through woods dominated by pine and hemlock and is split into two or more channels for close to a mile. The area, of course, exists today and offers a good example of what the forests of this region must have resembled before the lumbering operations of early settlers. Only little evidence of former farming exists along the West Branch between Cooleyville and Enfield, mostly on the east side. This may still be seen in the Dickeyville area and for a short distance above Rattlesnake Ledges in Prescott. On the west side of the valley evidence of former fields exists where Camel Brook enters the stream, below where Cobb Brook enters, and again near the entry of Atherton Brook. There was, of course, a scattering of farms higher up the hillside. Their remains are evident by the stone walls and the presence of old field pine. Occasionally a farm field has survived the encroachment of forest or planting carried out by MDC foresters during the 1930s and 1940s.

Just prior to closing of the area in the mid 1930s for clearing of the forest in connection with the Quabbin Reservoir, only two farmers remained in the bottom land on the west side of the river. They were Tom Cadwick and Myron Pierce. Both men lived alone, although Tom had descendants living elsewhere. Pierce had apparently remained a bachelor all his life. Like most residents of the three branches of Swift River Valley, they shared a strong reluctance to leave, and Cadwick, at least, was more outspoken than others in his opposition to being removed. The site of Pierce's farm is now under water, but Cadwick's is just above reservoir level and commands a magnificent view down the lake. It is situated just east of the very lower end of Atherton Brook, known to most trout fishermen of the early 1900s as Cadwick Brook. Tom Cadwick's fields are still in evidence just opposite Rattlesnake Ledges. Early in the century, the pitch pine was becoming more prevalent down the valley from Cadwick's, although the white pine was still the more commonly seen. A greater growth of oaks and other hardwoods was also present than farther upstream. I recall Tom Cadwick's farm with its low one-and-a-half-story house set against a hill. Several fields lay south of the house affording an exceptional view down the valley and to Rattlesnake Ledges on Prescott Hill. I have a fair recollection of Tom, although I was only four or five years old at the time. I was most struck with his usually grizzled and somewhat wild appearance. He had a pigpen in his yard, and I remember pulling up grass and feeding it to the pigs.

One Sunday when I was small, I waited with my mother in our 1926 Hudson touring car parked not far from Tom's house while my father fished. I particularly remember the wide place on the dirt road where we parked. The mosquitoes were bothersome that day, so my mother had stuffed sections of the newspaper around all but the windshield and back covering to keep them out. Then she settled to read the rest of the paper.

Mildred Foye and the 1926 Hudson touring car

Suddenly, a grizzled, startling face peered in at her. It was Tom, but my mother had no idea who he was. Tom knew that, in spite of Prohibition, my father generally had a bottle of rum or whiskey in the car—he claimed it warded off a cold on wet days. There were no locked compartments in cars in those days, and Tom was in the habit of helping himself to a shot or two while my father was downstream fishing.

There was also a .38 caliber revolver in the car. The instant she saw Tom, my mother grabbed the gun from the pocket and waved it in his face. Tom immediately burst out laughing, slapping his thigh in country fashion. Then he introduced himself. I have no recollection of whether Tom had his "drink" that day, but I suspect that when my father heard about the incident later, he offered Tom his accustomed shot.

A farm below the junction of the West Branch and Camel Brook was acquired in the late Teens by a recent immigrant who could not yet speak much English. On seeing two fishermen in the brook bordering on his land, he ran down the bank, yelling at them in a foreign tongue. One of the fishermen, Oscar Stacy, was an excellent pistol shot and carried a revolver with him while fishing. Considering the incidence of illegal removal of trout from the West Branch in those days, it may have been a wise practice. When the excited farmer reached the edge of the stream, Stacy placed a well-aimed shot in the water at his feet. The farmer ran back uphill just as rapidly—and decidedly more excited.

On another afternoon when my father was fishing with Oscar Stacy, they took refuge from a thunderstorm in a North Prescott farmhouse. While sitting around the kitchen with the farm family, they witnessed an incident that might have ended differently for a cat perched on the metal sink. Lightning struck behind the house and very close to the well—close enough that a sizable charge of electricity traveled up the pipe to the sink. The cat let out a howl and flew across the room in a shower of sparks. It survived without any visible damage but thereafter sought another vantage point in the kitchen.

On a July day in 1937 when I was in my early teens, I bicycled from Athol to fish the West Branch near where the Pierce farm had been. The house had been mostly torn down in anticipation of flooding the reservoir, and I left my bicycle behind a large maple near the house. It was well out of sight of the road. When I returned from fishing, the bicycle was gone. I could not imagine how anyone could have found it, but fortunately they left my sneakers. I changed from my boots to the sneakers and prepared for the long walk to the highway and, hopefully, a ride home. Just before leaving, I heard voices from the cellar and walked quietly over to the house. I tiptoed down the stairs. I was able to peer through a crack in the wall and saw two rough looking men eating a meal. I listened for a while but heard no mention of the bicycle. They were not men I would care to question, so I tiptoed out of there. Apparently, the two men were woodcutters employed to clear the area for flooding. They had taken up residence in Myron's cellar, the floor above serving as a roof.

I started walking up the dirt road that traversed the West Branch valley. After a short distance, I was picked up by couple of surveyors. When they heard my story, they drove me to Stowell's store in New Salem, where I could phone home. As soon as my father heard the details of the apparent theft, he came immediately—with a rifle. We pulled into the Pierce front yard just behind a truck with someone who was either picking up the two woodcutters or had returned from disposing of my bicycle. He hadn't turned off the truck when the two came out of the cellar. Seeing my father with rifle in hand, they hastily joined their friend in the truck. As they did, my father questioned them about the bicycle. Of course, they said they had not seen it. Not waiting for my father to move his car from the driveway, they sped out of there by cutting across the nearby field.

My father was determined to learn the identity of the men and try to recover the bicycle. The New Salem policeman Mr. Cox learned who the men were and that they came from a small town in the Berkshires. The following Sunday, we drove out there, where my father reported the theft to the chief of police. He informed us that the two had a very poor reputation and most likely had sold the bicycle at once. My father's determination was satisfied to some extent, and the chief dissuaded him from another confrontation with the two "villains."

He also did not buy me another bicycle. From then on, he transported me to and from the streams I wanted to fish. Stories of other Quabbin workmen driving though the half-deserted towns at night, firing off guns in Western style, were coming out of the Valley then. Despite the potential for theft and violence, my father did not warn me against fishing in the Valley streams—but neither did he want me riding around the area on a bicycle. After that incident, I did not fish those streams without at least one companion.

Two aspects of the environment of the West Branch below Cooleyville that greeted fishermen and nature lovers were the aroma and coolness in summer. In spring, the odor of new growth, damp ground, and swamp was overwhelming. In summer, under drier conditions, the pines emitted a pitchy fragrance. Autumn also had its characteristic but stimulating odors associated with ripeness and decay. There was also a certain "wet dog" smell I have never been able to identify. Other tributaries of the Swift River share the same fragrant attributes in relatively undisturbed groves of mature forest. The coolness one felt in these groves, most noticeable on hot, sultry days, is experienced wherever the sun light is kept out and the moisture under the canopy of needles and leaves is retained. I should mention, as well, that the light in these groves in early evening positively fascinated Clive Edwards, a friend associated with the British film industry.

Downstream as far as Dickey Bridge, the brook was moderately rapid with a succession of pools twenty or thirty yards in length. The forest was mainly of hemlock groves, with a fair amount of pine, oaks, and maples. At Dickey Meadow, elms became interspersed, with a greater intrusion of other hardwoods. The brook along Dickey Meadow was quite rapid with much smaller pools. Below Dickey Bridge, the stream was noticeably slower, but there was sufficient current during the high water of late winter and spring to gouge out pools of five to six feet in depth. Between the more rapid stretches, over most of the remainder of the course of the stream to Enfield, were found long pools where water flowed over long, sloping gravel runs into deep quiet stretches. In some places, the pools were forty to sixty yards long. Farther down, above the marsh known as Pelham Pond or Pelham Hollow Pond, the pools were seventy-five yards or more in length. The water was exceptionally clear, and against the light colored sandy bottom, large schools of trout were quite visible.

In some pools, particularly in the area around Gerty's Bridge, schools of trout were described as ranging from several hundred to a thousand in number. They attracted not only a sizable number of trout fishermen, both fly and bait, but also poachers intent on removing as many fish as possible. Their methods included netting as well as the use of dynamite or quicklime to stun the fish. My father happened upon an occurrence, around the early Twenties, when a pool was covered with hundreds of dead or immobilized trout. Two poachers were attempting to drown the game warden, Denny Shea, who had apprehended them. When my father appeared with his .38 revolver, the poachers fled. My father, of course, had Denny's lifelong gratitude.

As a boy in the late Thirties, I can recall fishing some of the pools near Gerty's Bridge and finding very few trout in them. Poaching had evidently taken a tremendous toll. However, by 1940, the last year I saw areas of the West Branch now under the reservoir, the trout population had rebounded considerably, and schools of between fifty and a hundred trout were again visible. This area of the stream was known as Bobbin Hollow, since a small plant making wooden bobbins for sewing machines had operated there. Gerty's Bridge was also located in this hollow and was the only permanent bridge on the West Branch between Dickey Bridge, near Dickeyville, and the bridge in Pelham below Pelham Pond. Gerty was, according to hearsay, a bold and forthright individual who served meals to the fishermen. Her characteristic reply when asked what she had to eat was "Vittles."

With huge pines, hardwoods, the tall fern growth of the valley, and the placid aspect of the stream, the area between the bridges had great beauty. The bottom was bright and sandy with green underwater plants in the shallows. It was a fly fisherman's delight because it was possible to make long casts under overarching trees to reach schools of trout in deeper water. The rush of water itself was a mere whisper near Gerty's Bridge, but I associate another sound more closely with the vicinity. I can still hear the whining of gears as my father shifted his Hudson into low when we pitched into Bobbin Hollow from Prescott Hill on the steep dirt roads leading down to the bridge. Deer jumping across the road in the dusk looked enormous, and I always stood up in the front of the car—there was plenty of room in those days—to see them better.

At a section of the stream known as Cadwick's, the flow was much more rapid and emitted a continuous soothing roar. The water rushed around bend pools and over huge embedded logs to deep drop offs in the sandy bed. Deep, dark holes lay where water swirled against tree trunks growing out from the bank. Varying from year to year, the pools were subject to great change from the high waters of late winter and early spring. Where one pool had been filled with gravel, another had been created, which gave much variety and expectation each spring to the fishing. Just above this stretch, from Myron Pierce's to Cadwick's, the flow was slower, but even there the pools would become filled and new ones appear. There were also stretches where the stream became filled with sand in the center but had deep runs along the banks, making for easier wading than in the Cadwick stretch. Of exceptional wildness, the whole Cadwick area of the valley was a land of magic and perilous wading to a boy. The sound of rushing water still carries with it for me a sense of excitement and great anticipation.

Between the Cadwick stretch and Bobbin Hollow was an area known as "The Jungle." The stream was fished very little in "The Jungle," the depth being too great for wading in most places. The bank and most of the valley at this point was crowded with a thick growth of stunted hardwoods, alders, and thorn-bushes, making it difficult to walk through, particularly if one were encumbered with a fishing rod and net. Overlooking the choked plain were the Rattlesnake Ledges of Prescott Hill. The growth indicates the plain must previously have been continuously flooded by beavers, and practically all large trees had been eliminated, in contrast to the river immediately above and below. "The Jungle" was also the home of otters; their fishing was seldom disturbed there. I recall an exhilarating encounter on a June day when I was fishing the deepening pools at the head of "The Jungle." Because I was not wearing boots, I was attempting to wade around the shallow side of a bend pool without getting in over my waist. To steady myself, I grabbed an alder branch that jutted over the water. I had the startling experience of seeing a black snake slither over my hand before dropping into the water just in front of me. After a few moments of immobility, I slowly backwatered out of there.

Although the West Branch was ideal for fly fishing, bait fishing was common, particularly by the farm boys of the area and other fishermen as well. Worms, salmon eggs, grasshoppers, and crickets were all used. Les Cooley, who grew up near Bobbin Hollow, claimed to catch the largest trout on live crickets he called "thunder bugs." Since the crickets are active at night, it might indicate the largest trout were caught at night. Trout weighing a pound and a half were caught regularly in Bobbin Hollow, with occasionally a two- or even three-pound trout. Considering that the average size of native brook trout in the eastern United States and Canada is from five to eight inches, brook trout over a pound—about thirteen and a half inches—are considered large and have probably been in the stream for six years or more. To my knowledge, no study of the rate of growth of trout in the cold waters of Swift River has been done, and no authenticated records exist of the size of the largest trout caught in the era before the reservoir.

Les Cooley was a friend of my father and is the source of information regarding the size of trout caught in the exceptionally clear and deep pools above and below Gerty's Bridge. Against the light colored sandy bottom, the trout in these pools were quite visible, and locating the larger ones was an easy matter. Cooley's fishing experience in this area predated the invasion by fly fishermen in the Teens, but his description of trout numbers and size pretty well match that of the early fly fishermen in the area. He was inducted into the Army and stationed at Camp Devens, at the same time as my father in 1918. My father had one of the few driving licenses among servicemen then and drove a truck for a time carrying the bodies of flu victims to the morgue. He had the saddening task of carrying Les's body.

One bait fisherman who was often a part of the scene in Bobbin Hollow in the Teens was Fred Stratton of Athol. Fred always fished in the same spot, sitting against the same tree, in the deep pool below Gerty's Bridge. He used a sixteen-foot cane pole and a worm baited hook dangling in the depths, six or seven feet. Fred kept every trout that he caught regardless of size, and when kidded about keeping "short trout," he remarked that his woman wouldn't let him throw the little ones back. I can picture Fred sitting in "his spot" in those peaceful surroundings, smoking his pipe. His woman also wouldn't let him smoke in the house. Fred was a Civil War veteran who had the habit of kicking

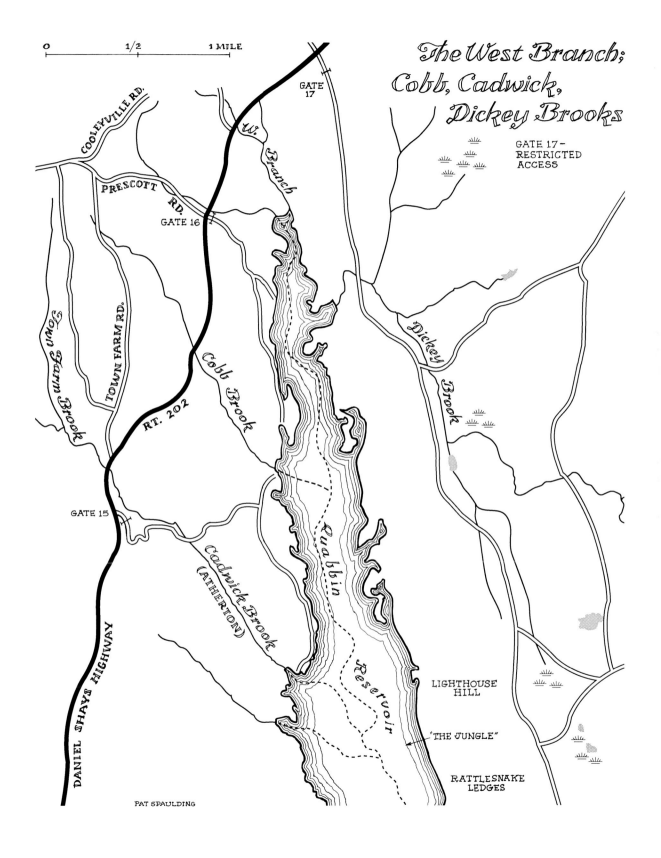

The West Branch; Cobb, Cadwick, Dickey Brooks

0   1/2   1 MILE

GATE 17 –
RESTRICTED
ACCESS

COOLEYVILLE RD.

W. Branch

GATE 17

PRESCOTT RD.

GATE 16

Dickey Brook

Town Farm Brook

TOWN FARM RD.

Cobb Brook

RT. 202

GATE 15

Cadwick Brook
(ATHERTON)

Quabbin

Reservoir

DANIEL SHAYS HIGHWAY

LIGHTHOUSE
HILL

"THE JUNGLE"

RATTLESNAKE
LEDGES

PAT SPAULDING

his heels into the air whenever he fell flat on the ground to take cover under fire. In one engagement, the inevitable happened, and one heel caught a .50 caliber slug of lead. Most likely the encounter affected his ability to walk for any great distance and explains why he never got very far from the bridge in his later years.

Below Bobbin Hollow was the large marsh called Pelham Pond. Although a natural marsh, it had been dammed to run a mill for a time. Fishing in Pelham Pond required a boat and was described as "damnably good" in the various bays and channels of the upper end of the marsh. For a fisherman addicted to the obstacles and challenges of stream fishing, however, pond fishing from a boat is much less exciting. It may be described as "just fishing," without the beautiful surroundings of the stream or the hazards to casting provided by tree, bush, log, or rock.

Below Pelham Pond, the West Branch was a sizable stream and could be waded only at the head of the long sloping runs leading into the deep pools or at the foot of the pool. The river to Enfield was flanked more by hardwoods, tall maples, and oaks, than by the mainly coniferous forests above Pelham Pond. The river was much slower for the most part with occasional faster stretches that gave out a low musical hum. Rapid stretches were populated by large numbers of smaller trout, five to six inches in length. Larger trout were found in deeper pools, but the stream from Pelham Pond to Enfield did not have the reputation for holding large trout that the Bobbin Hollow waters had. As the river approached Enfield, it ran through open, sometimes marshy meadows. It was much easier fly casting in such an open stretch and also permitted bait fishing with the long cane poles used early in the century. It also attracted more fishermen.

Below the junction of the West with the combined East and Middle branches at Enfield, the water became too warm to support the thriving trout populations of colder waters above. Although there may have been springs or cold inlets that harbored trout below the junction, I do not recall hearing that it was good trout water. Today, with cold water released from the bottom of the reservoir at Winsor Dam, the river supports trout for some distance below. Well stocked with trout, it also supports a sizable population of fishermen but does not attract those of us who prefer to fish in wilder surroundings.

Camel, Cobb, Cadwick (Atherton) Brooks

Most tributaries of the West Branch below Cooleyville flow in from the west side, with the exception of Dickey Brook. Rocky Run, which enters the stream north of Cooleyville, is too small to be considered fishable but provides refuge for fingerlings. Camel and Cobb Brooks are also too small for fly fishermen, but that part of Camel in the flood plain of the West Branch supports trout as much as six or seven inches in length. Cobb Brook is large enough for the bait fisherman and drops into the West Branch valley over some scenic cascades and falls. In the very upper reaches of this little brook, it meanders along a relatively flat valley where in late August unusually large numbers of the cardinal flower may be seen.

Cadwick Brook has a much greater length than either Camel or Cobb and has a sizable population of small native trout. Its source is two rivulets. One of them is called Town Farm Brook, probably from the fact that it originates near a former town farm, or poor house, in Shutesbury. A diminutive stream, it has a sizable population of fingerlings as does the upper end of Cadwick. They can be seen darting in the slow water only inches deep. The forest near Town Farm Brook, on high ground, is a relatively mature hardwood growth composed of maple, oak, birch, and ash. The forest floor is heavily populated with ferns and allows for few wild flowers. The gypsy moth conflagration of 1979 to 1981 did much damage to the oaks, but an appreciable number nevertheless survived.

After the slow flow of the brook below the two upper branches, it drops rapidly for the rest of its course to the reservoir, a distance of three hundred ten feet over two miles. The flow is usually over a series of miniature falls, but there is one spectacular falls just above the road that goes down the hill from Gate 14. With a bed of light colored rocks and sand, the stream in some stretches is flanked by rock outcrops on the steep slopes of the very narrow valley or gorge through which it flows. Such gorges in the Swift River watershed and surrounding areas are often referred to as "hemlock gutters," a rather inelegant term for such striking scenery. As well as exceptionally tall hemlocks and pines are some hardwoods, mainly oak, birch, and maple. When morning or afternoon sun slants through the majestic trees, it creates an aspect of great beauty.

A dam in relatively good condition, though washed out at one end, still stands just above the bridge on the road running downhill from Gate 14. Also, stone abutments of a former bridge may be seen just above the Daniel Shays highway. The remains of a millpond are visible just where the stream enters the reservoir, but the dam must have been mainly of wood because no trace remains. The pond is located west of the Cadwick farmhouse and above the road that traversed the west side of the valley. Below the road, the brook took a last rapid drop into the valley, where it became a deep, slow moving stream.

Dickey Brook

DICKEY BROOK IS THE ONLY STREAM ON THE EAST SIDE of the West Branch valley large enough to be considered trout water. It originates in several branches on the north slope of Prescott Hill and has a northerly course for much of its length. The branches join in a marshy area of Atkinson Hollow, now a succession of beaver ponds. Below the marsh, the brook falls rapidly over dark colored stones and ledges, unlike lighter colored rocks of the upper West Branch or Cadwick Brook. Where the brook reaches the plain of the West Branch valley, its course turned west, then southerly, and the bottom was of the same sand and gravel as the rest of the West Branch. Dickey Brook supported a large population of native trout, in size up to about three quarters of a pound. Larger trout that survived probably sought the deeper waters of West Branch. With the warming of the water by beaver ponds in the upper reaches of the brook, the trout population has declined.

The stone foundation of a mill remains in relatively good condition in the Dickeyville area, just at the point where the brook enters the reservoir when the reservoir is full. Across the road, a diversion from considerably upstream is still visible. It is located just above the junction of the stream with a branch from the north. The northerly branch flows out of a sizable marsh at times and in various places dammed by beavers. Remains of a stone dam also exist just below the marshy area on the main branch of Dickey Brook below Atkinson's Hollow, but no evidence of a mill is there today. Another stone foundation is also found farther upstream at the junction of two branches, but what it supported is questionable, since the brook has only enough fall to keep it barely moving at that point. The brook has a fall of about one hundred eighty feet, starting at the junction of the two main branches at Atkinson's Hollow to the West Branch valley, a distance of about two miles.

An amusing incident occurred in the 1920s just above the junction of Dickey Brook with the West Branch. A farmer living there had a large belligerent dog that dissuaded some fishermen from fishing his stretch of stream, then in an open meadow. A fisherman had just bought a new car and did not want the dog anywhere nearby. He informed his companions he would "take care" of that dog with a well aimed spit of tobacco juice. When the dog ran up to the car as usual, the fisherman let fly. In anticipation of this mixed moment of satisfaction and revenge, however, the fisherman forgot to roll down the window. The new car received an internal christening with tobacco juice.

Nearby, where the road just skirts the hill on the north side of the brook between Dickeyville and Dickey Bridge is a small stone enclosure built into the side of the hill. It is about twelve feet wide, ten feet deep, and about five feet high. It possibly served as the rear of a cooling shed, although it is in an exposed location today and must have been more shaded before. A similar stone structure is found on the west side of West Branch just up the valley from Dickey Meadow where the brook flowed close to the hillside. A more extensive example with three sides stoned in is located on the old road from Cooleyville to Millington, just where South Main Street in New Salem joins it. The roof over the structure still existed up to the early 1970s.

Other brooks flowing into West Branch from the west side as far south as Enfield, include Cadwell Creek and Briggs, Purgee, and Gulf brooks. They are too small to be considered fishable trout water, but they probably all serve as spawning grounds and havens for trout fry. No doubt on the plain before entering the West Branch, they had pools deep enough to support mature trout, particularly Cadwell. Like other small brooks flowing into the branches of Swift River, their trout populations were made up mainly of fry and fingerlings. After reaching five or six inches in length, trout settled into the main branches of the river. Most of the brooks are quite scenic as they flow rapidly downhill in a succession of miniature falls.

Among more spectacular plants growing in Swift River watershed streams may be cited marsh marigold, which blooms in early May. Pickerel weed and arrowhead are generally not found because of the rapid flow of the streams, but they did, of course, exist in the ponds of the Middle Branch. In August, the brook lobelia is common, followed by the sublime cardinal flower. The cardinal flower, whose striking beauty fits the grand surroundings, finds a foothold in quiet pockets or pools where mud has been allowed to accumulate and the current does not ever become too swift. As it is scattered along the streams infrequently, it is interesting that the plant manages to propagate itself at such wide intervals.

Another plant growing along the streams is the false hellebore. I prefer the official designation of *Veratrum viride*, which suggests both the vivid green of the plant when young and the toxic nature of the alkaloids in its foliage and roots. The plant has an air of fatality: after a brilliant display of greenery in its early life and an overabundance of fruit, it dies an early death in late June or early July. It becomes a wilting brown, followed by total collapse when the surrounding vegetation is still at its most vigorous.

Transportation to the streams in days before the automobile came into common use required planning. Fishermen from Athol who wished to spend a day on the West Branch above or below Cooleyville often went in groups of three or four. A horse and wagon, or "team" as it was referred to, was hired, and the party set out about midnight. They kept a very leisurely pace to Cooleyville, or other destination, and with the exception of the driver, were able to get a little sleep, or at least relaxation, on the way. It was probably the superior eyesight of the horse that kept them on the road in those unlit times. After arriving at the section of stream they planned to fish, one fisherman was dropped off and given a mile or so to fish. Then a second one started his stretch for another mile or more, and so on to the point where the last fisherman started his stretch of stream. At this point, the horse was tethered and left until fishermen from upstream had arrived. When they had all reached the team, they drove down the road bordering the stream to the quitting place of the last fisherman, and they picked him up. If there was enough daylight left, they might stop at a pond on the way back to Athol. Usually, arrival time in Athol was around the following midnight.

When automobiles became available to the trout fishermen of the Teens, the trip to Cooleyville could still be arduous. From Athol, it was eighteen miles over narrow, hilly dirt roads. During the early season, April to June, the roads were often "soft." Carrying a load of stones was sometimes the resort in order to get through the wettest sections of road. Of course, there were numerous incidents when cars had to be pulled out of the mud by farmers' horses.

Breakdowns and flat tires were also common with cars of the era. My father described one rather slow return to Athol at night from West Branch at a time when the roads were "good." On one rough section, the headlights broke, but he was able to keep the car on the road by staying under the rather narrow strip of starlit sky visible between the canopy of trees on either side of the road. It was also quickly evident when the car started to lean into the ditch on either side. Using both of these indicators, he was able to stay on the road. It must have been an exhausting ride.

42/Trout Waters

Standing in a riffle on West Branch

Middle Branch meanders toward "The Bulkhead"

The Middle Branch

THE MIDDLE BRANCH HAS ITS SOURCE IN NUMEROUS RIVULETS in the northwest corner of New Salem and the southeast corner of Wendell. One of the westerly tributaries starts in a pond that was once a marshy meadow less than half a mile from the source of one branch of Canada Brook. The tributary flows into Porter's Pond, small and scenic with a dirt causeway crossing it. The place appears wild and primitive, and the causeway has afforded the growth of unexpectedly large white pines. Years ago, there were reports of trout caught in Porter's. In my experience, however, it has yielded only the usual regional pond fish— including some rather large hornpout.

Below Porter's Pond, the stream is quite diminutive. It becomes fishable trout water after it joins several other rivulets to form a slow, swampy section. The stream then starts its rapid, rocky course to Morse Village, where a good-sized millpond existed before the dam was destroyed by the Thirties' floods. Stone remains of this dam are still in evidence. In its day, the millpond was heavily fished for trout. Below it, the brook ran through an open field formerly open to fishermen and then into the forests above the falls at Bearsden. Only one slow section of the stretch is level enough to support a beaver pond. There is evidence of a former stone dam at the end of the stretch.

Below the wild and sometimes roaring Bearsden cascades, the brook continues its rapid, rocky course to the marshy meadows of Toad Hollow. The remains of another stone dam are just below Bearsden: when a pond existed at this point, it supported a significant population of trout. Between the dam and Toad Hollow, there was a rather deep pool with good shelter from overhanging roots. A sizable trout was known to inhabit it sometime in the 1920s. Many area trout fishermen attempted to catch the fish, and I think it tells much of their sporting qualities that the fish was finally caught on fly by strictly conventional practice. It may occur to some that the trout should be easy prey to a worm or other bait, but I have seen many instances when large brook trout have passed up worms and other live bait but succumbed to a well placed artificial fly.

Toad Hollow was formerly a popular stretch for bait fishermen. It had a heavy growth of alders that allowed few spots for fly casting, although it became open enough in the very lower end of the marsh. Most of the upper reaches of this marsh have been spoiled as trout water by small beaver dams causing sand and mud to build up in formerly deep pools. The lower end of the marsh,

45

however, retains its former depth and still supports a trout population. A section below the Toad Hollow bridge splits into many relatively inaccessible branches that probably still hold trout.

In a relatively shallow section of the stretch below the bridge, with firmer footing than in the rest of the marsh, is the crossing of the Hessian Road. Still visible just south of Swift River Valley Historical Society buildings in North New Salem, the road was used by captured Hessian troops to march to Boston after they surrendered at Bennington, Vermont, in 1777. I have learned from former residents of the Valley that some Hessians later returned to settle. Others were given land by the British government in Lunenburg County, Nova Scotia. Their descendants are still there, in many cases on their original grants of one hundred sixty acres.

Toad Hollow brings me back to my very early fly fishing days. My father told me there was a spring seeping into the brook just below a spot known as the Bulkhead located at the point where Daniel Shays Highway now crosses the stream. The spring kept a small area of stream cooler than the rest, and my father instructed me to approach the pool cautiously, allow the fly to settle almost to the bottom, and pull it slowly to the surface. I followed his directions with great anticipation and was rewarded by a gentle tug. The hook was set, and I eventually landed a beautifully colored "brookie" weighing close to a half pound. It was not a trophy trout by any means, but everything happened according to expectation, and that was most impressive to a young mind. I remember that trout although many others of much larger dimensions have slipped from memory. Or perhaps, as Byron writes, "The time of our youth is the time of our glory."

From Porter's Pond to Toad Hollow, the Middle Branch drops four hundred thirty feet over a distance of about three miles. Except for a short stretch below Keystone Bridge where there were rapids for a couple hundred yards, the stream flowed more slowly below Toad Hollow. Keystone Bridge near Gate 30 is named, of course, for its construction. Made entirely of hand fitted stones, it is still serviceable today. After the short rapids, Middle Branch flowed through a boggy meadow, undoubtedly the site of former beaver ponds. Then it went through an extensive area of shallows that widened in places nearly to pond dimensions.

Black ducks populated this wider area, and some fishermen returned in the fall to hunt them. One who both fished and hunted this part of the stream was Ernest Horton, an Athol-Orange area electrician who was still working fulltime and was remarkably spry at the age of eighty-five. He had a shotgun so heavy that he called it "the old sink spout." Below the shallows, the brook became deep and slow. It was excellent trout water.

Near the stone abutments of an old bridge at the head of this stretch, a small tributary called Spriggy Brook flowed in. I learned from my father that his father and others fished Spriggy Brook around the turn of the century. Today the brook above the reservoir is quite diminutive, but before entering the Middle Branch, it was once wide and deep enough to allow the bait fishing carried on at the time. The brook then flowed through open fields, and these were the places most often fished. Their tackle usually consisted of a very small reel and a sixteen foot cane pole with small eyelets to carry a thin line. Fishermen stood well back from the bank and lowered a baited hook into deeper spots. After a trout had time to swallow the hook, it was flung out of the water, often landing twenty or thirty feet back in the field. Trout in small meadow streams like Spriggy Brook probably rarely exceeded eight inches in length, but they were so numerous that fishermen were able to "fill the basket" in an afternoon. With the advent of fly fishing early in the Teens, the cane pole bait fishing technique was pretty much abandoned except by farm boys. With fly fishing, larger and more wooded streams that required long casting became fishable.

The conservation philosophy of state officials responsible for fish and game laws that emerged sometime in the Twenties resulted in closing the small tributaries to fishing. The idea was that feeder streams would serve as breeding grounds and provide trout for larger streams. The practice was later abandoned, and small feeder streams were reopened to fishing. The six-inch legal size limit that had existed previously was also abandoned when the feeder streams were reopened. Unfortunately, the policy allowed the taking of small trout that should have been left in the streams as a breeding population. The toll on such streams has been particularly heavy in the fall, just prior to the time that trout breed. Fall fishing is a recent development providing many pleasant days on the stream, but more protection should be provided for smaller streams and their breeding trout which are generally no more than five or six inches in length.

Small brooks still serve their purpose as spawning areas, and numbers of fingerlings may be observed in some of them. Larger trout also survive in tiny streams, and with the cover provided from branches above and logs below, they are almost impossible to catch. I heard of a woodcutter who discovered a ten-inch trout in a spring hole not much larger than the fish. Crawling up to the hole on his belly, he succeeded in catching the trout on a worm.

About three miles below Keystone was Winter Bridge, situated near the base of Rattlesnake Hill. The Middle Branch from Keystone Bridge down was known to trout fishermen as Buffalo Brook, and the stretch between the two bridges was considered a day of fishing. Below Winter Bridge, the stream was slow, deep, and often impossible for wading. The forest along Middle Branch was less dominated by pine and hemlock groves than that of the West Branch. Maple, birch, ash, and oak were more prevalent. There were areas with extensive pine groves in the Middle Branch valley, but along the river there was a greater prevalence of hardwoods. The stretch of stream immediately below Winter Bridge was not suitable for fly casting because of the brook's brushy borders. Also, much of it had to be fished from the bank. When the stream entered the bed of the former Thompson Pond, however, the bottom became sandy, and the banks were inhabited mainly by alders. Long casting was therefore possible, providing excellent fly fishing to the point that the pond bed became too soft to be maneuverable. Thompson Pond trout were like the light colored, beautifully spotted fish found in the West Branch; trout caught from the Toad Hollow meadows and below were much darker. West Branch tributaries with dark rock bottoms also produced dark trout.

Below Thompson Pond, the Middle Branch became too warm to support trout. There were spots likely fed by springs or small tributaries farther down the valley, however, where trout were occasionally caught. When the Quabbin Reservoir was filling in the early Forties, the MDC closed the whole area to fishing. Some fishermen continued to fish the closed waters and were apprehended by MDC police. In court, local judges generally imposed a fine of five dollars for "trespass," as the charge was then called. Fishermen who were "caught" stated it was worth the five dollars to fish there, since sizable strings of trout—and some large specimens of two pounds or more—were taken. According to reports of the wardens, the largest trout of the three branches of Swift River were caught in the Middle Branch. My assumption is that most of the larger fish came from the water above and below Winter Bridge, which had been so difficult to fish.

After several seasons of chasing out trespassing fishermen in the Quabbin area, the MDC decided that fishing would be impossible to prevent. Local judges were no longer accepting Quabbin "trespass" cases in their dockets. On

July 1, 1946, specified areas of the Quabbin, both reservoir and tributaries, were "opened" to fishing. The situation exists to the present.

Brook, brown, lake, and rainbow trout as well as salmon have been stocked at various times in the reservoir. Relatively good fishing has thus been provided not only for these species but also for the pond fish that were previously present in valley ponds. Perch, pickerel, bluegills, pumpkinseeds, various species of bass, and hornpout are among the varieties still present.

Moosehorn Brook

ORIGINATING IN BOGS AND BEAVER PONDS in northeastern New Salem, the main branch of Moosehorn Brook starts close to the Wendell town line. Depending on the needs of the beavers, the now bog/then pond furthest upstream is in the same locale as the origins of the West and Middle branches of Swift River. It is within a mile of Porter's Pond. A glacial lake likely existed in the now boggy upland, and brooks are still spilling out of it on the north, east, and south sides.

For most of its course from source to junction with Manning Brook, Moosehorn Brook is a small, downhill rivulet with a drop of three hundred ten feet over about two miles. Although too small and overhung for fly casting, it has always been a spot for bait fishermen. The average size of trout in this stretch of brook is not much over six inches. After Moosehorn joins with Manning Brook, it flows through a series of abandoned beaver ponds. Formerly overgrown with alders and other swamp-loving woody plants, Moosehorn below Manning was practically impossible to fish by any method. To anyone with sufficient curiosity and ability for crouching and crawling through the alders, however, trout could be seen darting wherever a view of the sandy bottom could be obtained. In one small pool just above where the brook now enters the reservoir, I recall having seen trout covering the entire bottom of the pool. From the bridge on the old Moosehorn Road to Moosehorn Pond, the brook was large enough for bait fishing. Some stretches, however, were too overgrown for use of even a telescopic rod and a worm. The bottom of the stream was sandy for the most part with various water plants in the summer, and trout had the brilliant colors found in streams of this type. Apparently in the early days of the century, there was some open meadow land along the stream, and it was a favorite of fishermen of the era.

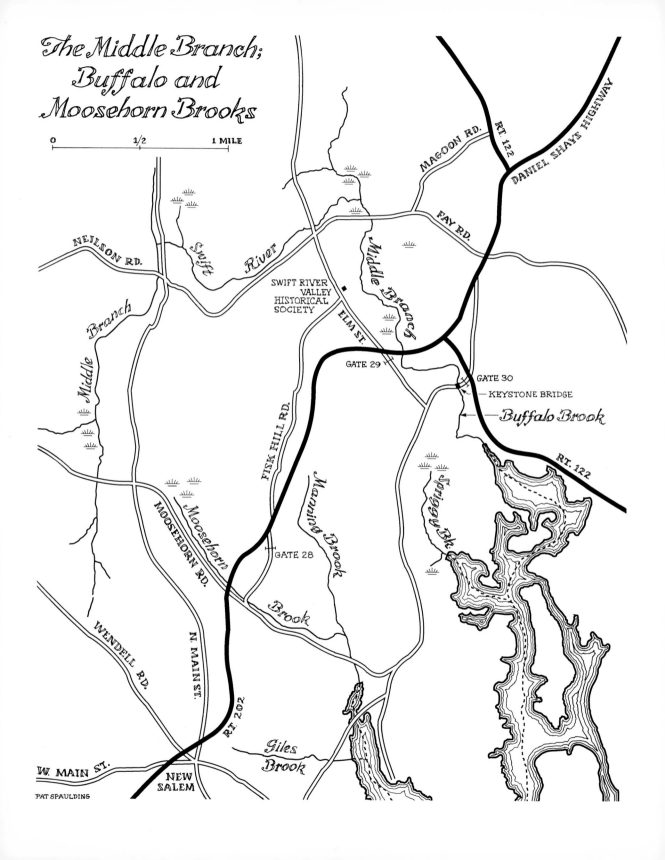

The Middle Branch;
Buffalo and
Moosehorn Brooks

0   1/2   1 MILE

NEILSON RD.

Swift River

Middle Branch

SWIFT RIVER
VALLEY
HISTORICAL
SOCIETY

Middle

Branch

MAGOON RD.

RT. 122

DANIEL SHAYS HIGHWAY

FAY RD.

Middle Branch

ELM ST.

GATE 29

GATE 30

KEYSTONE BRIDGE

Buffalo Brook

RT. 122

FISK HILL RD.

Manning Brook

Sprigay Bk.

GATE 28

Moosehorn

MOOSEHORN RD.

N. MAIN ST.

Brook

WENDELL RD.

RT. 202

Giles
Brook

W. MAIN ST.

NEW
SALEM

PAT SPAULDING

In days before automobiles were commonly used, fishermen from Athol would plan a day of trout fishing on Moosehorn Brook in the morning and on Middle Branch in the afternoon. They started by taking the early morning train, known as "The Rabbit" because of its numerous short runs, to New Salem Station and walking across the flat plain to Millington. The plain supported some very tall pines along the road. The walk beneath them in the early morning light must have been exhilarating, combined with the high expectations normal to all true fishermen.

They started their fishing just west of Millington at Moosehorn Pond. Usually they went in groups of four or five, so it did not take very long to cover a couple miles of stream. They generally fished only the more open and inviting pools. The day's fishing went well up Moosehorn, close to its boggy source, and the party then walked the short distance to Porter's Pond. Lunch was probably taken at this spot, along with an "hour's nooning," as a midday rest was referred to then. The group then fished down Middle Branch to the Toad Hollow meadows. I believe they were usually picked up there by a friend with a horse and wagon. Another eight-mile walk after that day's excursion would have been more of a feat than even the most avid of trout fishermen today would be willing to make in pursuit of his sport.

Because of the relatively slow flow in the valley below the junction with Manning Brook, there were no suitable sites for mills. One dammed pond did exist just below the road leading up to New Salem Center, but it may have served farm animals rather than a mill wheel. The drop in elevation from the junction with Manning Brook to Moosehorn Pond was sixty-six feet over a distance of about three miles. Manning, I should add, is much too small for fishing by today's views, but farm boys fished this brook and others equally diminutive. In the late 1800s and early 1900s, however, many brooks flowed through open fields that provided good insect feed for trout. Fishing was also easy for the boys because the open meadow brooks were unencumbered by brush.

Tyre Brook

THE STREAM COMMONLY DESIGNATED ON MAPS AS HOP BROOK was known to the trout fishing community of the late 1800s and early 1900s as Tyre. When stocking trout by the state became annual practice in the 1920s and 1930s, it was

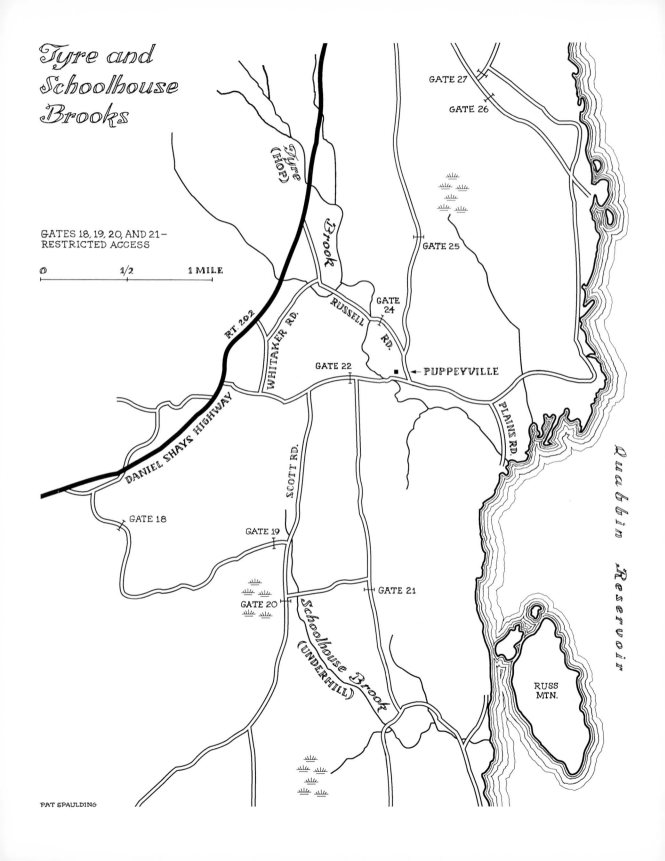

designated in lists of stocked streams as Tyre Brook. How the brooks in this and other areas were named, when not for an early settler living on their banks, make interesting stories. In a number of cases, the brooks of the Swift River watershed had more than one name, and different sections of a brook would sometimes have different names. It is quite possible that Tyre and Hop originally referred to different stretches of the stream. In any event, I much prefer the name Tyre for this beautiful stream. Biblical names were commonly used as first names by early settlers, and it seems appropriate that names for some brooks of the region should allude to the Bible. The name Hop is much too prosaic for this colorful stream. One of the few dyes for clothing before the advent of the dye industry in the late 1800s was called Tyrian Purple, obtained from a mollusk found in the Mediterranean Sea. It was used by the royalty of European kingdoms for their gowns, and the allusion also seems appropriate for the brook.

Tyre Brook originates in springs and rivulets in the high land of northwest New Salem. One branch, however, starts just west of the village, and although barely noticeable today, it was fished in earlier times by village boys. Several tiny tributaries of this brook come together in the two main branches that join just below the Daniel Shays Highway. With the exception of a couple of boggy areas, they flow down hill rapidly. One boggy area was formerly a millpond just off West Main Street. After the two branches join, the brook flows comparatively slowly through a lushly vegetated valley dominated by tall maples and oaks and, in some sections, the ever recurring pine and hemlock. Dense stands of ferns mark the area: hay-scented, New York, lady, and the great osmundas, all interspersed with bracken. Roughly to the bridge in what was once Puppeyville, the stream had many areas of light colored sand or gravel bottom contrasted with areas where the stream flowed over dark colored rocks. Sandy stretches most likely originated from the presence of beaver ponds. This section of the stream also has unexpected twists and turns, probably formed by previous beaver dams. With the recent redamming of the stream by beavers and the breaking of dams by high water after ponds were abandoned, some of these turns have disappeared. A recent invasion of beavers has left fringes and groves of dead tree trunks that provide living space for birds and mammals that dwell in hollow trees. Dead trees from beaver floodings are known to some as rampikes.

The beaver population in the area in and around the Quabbin watershed has been cited as one of the largest concentrations of beavers presently in this country. The return of beavers to the region occurred in the mid-1940s. By the mid-1950s, they had established their ponds on most of the brooks of the watershed. Some of the slower streams like Shattuck became a succession of beaver ponds. In general, the presence of beaver ponds has been of advantage to many forms of wildlife. However, where the water has become too warm for trout to survive because of the slower flow and loss of shade created by beaver activity, the trout have left for colder waters.

Beavers maintain their ponds as long as a supply of alders, willows, and saplings of both hardwoods and conifers are available for their diet of bark. When the food supply is exhausted in the immediate area of a pond, the beavers abandon it. The pond bed, which has become rich with silt during the beaver presence, quite often becomes a garden. Goldenrod, asters, jewel weed, bone set, steeple bush, and meadowsweet are common in such ensilted areas. Decaying beaver dams frequently support a population of mint and marsh St. John's wort. Gradually, however, alders and willows return to crowd out the plants, and beavers will return to reflood the area and cut alders and willows when they have become sufficiently numerous.

The drop in elevation from the westerly branch where it crosses West Main Street in New Salem to Puppeyville is three hundred eighty-four feet over a distance of two and a half miles. From Puppeyville Bridge to Plains Road Bridge, the drop is one hundred seventy feet over a distance of about a mile.

At Puppeyville, the remains of a rather large stone dam and mill site may be seen. There are stone embankments on the stream below the dam. Beavers periodically restore the pond by erecting a dam at the same site, using remains of the stone dam. Before the farmhouses of Puppeyville were removed to close the Quabbin reservation, the brook flowed through an open field. It was a favorite fishing spot for both bait and fly fishermen. Below the bridge, however, the bottom becomes rocky as the brook starts its racy downhill course to the Middle Branch valley.

Some abandoned Puppeyville fields grew into favored habitat for woodcock. Often when fishing this stretch, I wander through the coverts to see how many woodcock are summering there. They are sometimes found quite close to the brook as well. I was once surprised to have one fly up no more than six feet from my head. The bird had been perched on one of the stones of the embankment just below the old dam, a most unlikely place to find a woodcock.

One rather depressing incident comes to mind in connection with Puppeyville. I was fishing there with another schoolboy when the Quabbin area was being cleared for the reservoir. We took refuge from a heavy downpour in a house not yet completely dismantled. At least the roof was still intact. Scattered around the floor were many pieces of correspondence we read to pass the time before one of our fathers came to pick us up. From the letters, a number of which were evidently replies to requests for money or other assistance, we were able to piece together the sad attempts of the last family to live there to survive the Depression of the Thirties. It had a most sobering effect on our youthful enthusiasm, particularly when I recalled the spirited and pretty young girl I had seen fishing there a year or two earlier. She could very well have lived in that last house in Puppeyville.

Below Puppeyville, the stream starts its rocky, downhill course through a narrow, scenic gorge. Huge pines, hemlocks, oaks, maples, and birches of the "hemlock gutters" dominate. The stream flows over multicolored rocks and ledges, in some places creating small waterfalls. The whole effect of forest and stream, with fallen logs and overhanging trees, is one of wildness and nature undisturbed. Other such gorges are along Cadwick, Cobb, and Schoolhouse brooks. There is no indication that any was ever lumbered, probably because of the difficulty in getting logs up the steep sides. Existing in their precolonial splendor, they provide a majestic remnant of the post-glacial forests of the region.

One hot afternoon when I was fishing the exciting stretch of the stream below Puppeyville, I became curious as to what the water was like beneath a waterfall. I took off my clothes and swam up under one of the falls. I was surprised to find the water perfectly clear and quiet below what looked like a churning mass of foam and water from above. The falls was only four or five feet high, but foam was visible a few inches below the surface. Observing the clarity of the water explained the previous mystery of how trout feeding below these falls could detect the fly so quickly.

Perhaps the most scenic of the falls on Tyre Brook is at the site of the old Plains Road Bridge. Although the drop is only three or four feet, the pool below is spectacular because of its depth and light, sandy bottom. Below the pool, now near the shores of the Quabbin, the brook entered one last rocky, downhill rapid. Then it flowed more slowly through the sandy plain of Middle Branch. Wide and beautiful bend pools in the brook made fly casting a delight, and the trout were generally larger than in stretches upstream. Occasionally, open meadows bordered the brook and provided additional insect life for the trout's diet. With ferns overhanging the banks and towering hardwoods, this part of the

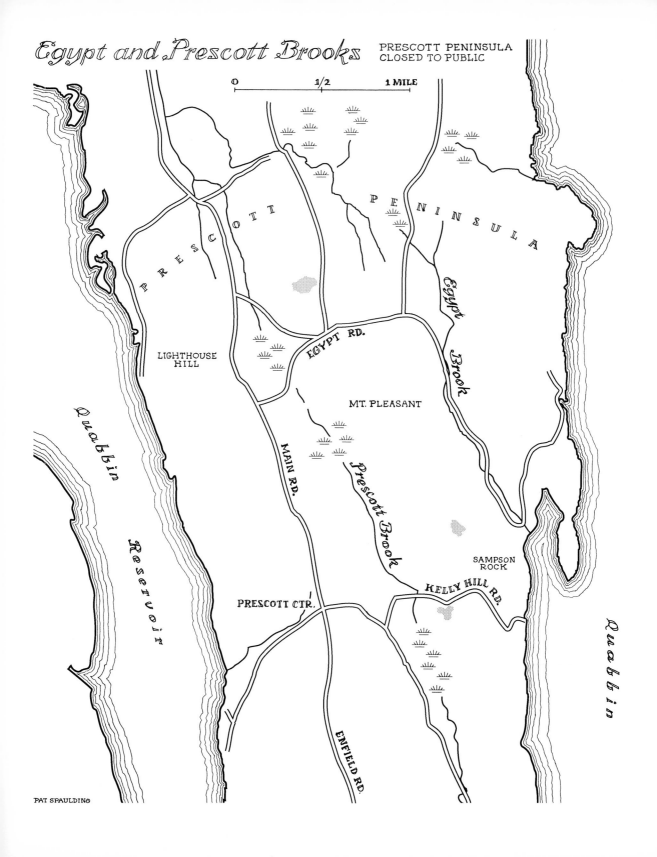

Egypt and Prescott Brooks

PRESCOTT PENINSULA
CLOSED TO PUBLIC

0   1/2   1 MILE

PRESCOTT

PENINSULA

Egypt Brook

LIGHTHOUSE
HILL

EGYPT RD.

MT. PLEASANT

Quabbin

Reservoir

MAIN RD.

Prescott Brook

SAMPSON
ROCK

KELLY HILL RD.

PRESCOTT CTR.

Quabbin

ENFIELD RD.

PAT SPAULDING

stream was equal in beauty to the rocky, wilder stretches above. Before the stream entered Moosehorn Pond, it flowed through a densely vegetated area reminiscent of "The Jungle" of the West Branch. In many ways, this was a somewhat smaller duplication of the West Branch in its Pierce and Cadwick stretches. It produced the same light colored but brilliantly spotted trout. Present day maps of Quabbin streams designate Moosehorn Pond as Hop Brook Pond, a name certainly not in common use previously.

Schoolhouse (Underhill), Egypt, Prescott Brooks

RUNNING INTO MIDDLE BRANCH FROM THE WEST, the next three brooks below Tyre flow in a southeasterly direction. They are quite small, from the fly fisherman's point of view, and for the most part are rapid downhill streams. The last stretches in the flat plain of the Middle Branch valley were probably most productive of trout large enough to catch and keep. Schoolhouse Brook, so called by fishermen because it started behind the schoolhouse in North Prescott, flowed into Woods Pond. On maps, Schoolhouse Brook is commonly labeled Underhill Brook. Located in the plain before entering the Middle Branch, Woods Pond often provided trout in the pound and a half class. I understand that fishing in this pond was not open to the public.

Schoolhouse Brook, although quite small, has several scenic waterfalls in its downhill course from North Prescott. All of these brooks have dashing rapids and deep pools among the tumbled rocks. For the most part, they do not support trout much over six inches, except in beaver ponds. Such ponds seem to attract trout almost overnight from the time they are built, and some of them eventually support trout of up to a pound or more. This was expected to be true of Prescott Brook, where a substantial boggy area east of Prescott Center exists. I recall meeting a couple of trespassing fishermen who had made the long hike into the lower rapid end of Prescott Brook several years after the reservoir had filled up in 1946. They were quite disgruntled over the size of the trout they caught, because hardly any exceeded six inches. Larger trout evidently went downstream into the reservoir once it was created and found larger tributaries for their spring and summer feeding grounds.

In the wild part of the Middle Branch valley below Tyre and above Egypt Brook—near Russ Mountain with its steep slopes and tall spires of ancient pines—two brothers from Athol set up a still during the Prohibition years. They apparently thought their operation would escape detection in that relatively uninhabited corner of Prescott, but they had the unfortunate experience of being apprehended. On the other hand, home-brewed beer was served openly in the bar of the Greenwich Inn several miles down the Valley to customers known to the proprietor.

Schoolhouse Brook had a length of only two miles from North Prescott to Woods Pond. Egypt had a length of two and a half miles from its boggy source to its junction with the Middle Branch. Prescott Brook was longest at three and a half miles from where it crossed the Prescott Center-Egypt Brook road to its junction with Middle Branch. The section of Egypt Brook on the plain was known to fishermen as Dollar Brook, because the farmer who owned the fields around the brook charged fishermen a dollar for access. It might have been worth this price to fish there during the high water of early spring, but by August the brook had dwindled to questionable fishability.

West Branch of Fever Brook

DESIGNATED THE WEST BRANCH OF FEVER BROOK ON MAPS, it was known either as Sputtermill or Blackmer Brook to fishermen of the area. It originates in a boggy area, once dammed, near the old Monson Turnpike in Petersham. Before the filling of Quabbin Reservoir, it joined the East Branch of Fever east of North Dana. For most of its course, Sputtermill is a boggy, slow stream but has short sections of rapids with miniature waterfalls and, in places, sizable pools. Many of the slow stretches are overgrown with alders and provide excellent cover for trout. In some areas, the stream widens to resemble small ponds. Sizable native trout of a pound or more formerly inhabited this stream. It has a drop in elevation of only two hundred feet from its source to its former junction with the East Branch of Fever, about four and a half miles.

In its present state, most of the boggy sections of the brook have become beaver flowages. This has warmed the water considerably, and probably due to the relatively large areas of the beaver ponds and the relatively small flow of water, the stream has become too warm for trout during the summer months. The once large population of brook trout has now dwindled to a few that appear during early spring and the fall months. The others probably left the brook, via the reservoir, to enter colder streams. State stocking of trout, however, has provided good spring fishing since the beavers invaded the stream in the early

1960s, and the stream became fairly acidic in the mid 1980s. Thus, the native fish population has declined. The acidity resulting from vegetative decay in the beaver ponds coupled with the increasing amount from rain and other atmospheric deposition apparently caused the present poor conditions for trout. This development has been most unfortunate, because the brook formerly provided good early season trouting for both bait and fly fishermen.

The boggy section of the brook at the base of Soapstone Hill was formerly known as the Old Beaver Hole. Since about 1962 or 1963, this has reverted to a beaver pond of good size and has been in almost continuous use by beavers since that time. Although the loss of trout from this part of the brook is to be regretted, the succession of beaver ponds has provided good habitat for waterfowl. Apparently, a population of rough fish like dace, suckers, and sunfish has become established in this pond, as evidenced by the presence of otters and minks, which find them palatable. It is a pleasure and education to watch the almost systematic fishing habits of otters and their astounding energy, but I can't say that I find the same delight in seeing the more sinister and sinuous tactics of minks. Perhaps the rather fun loving habits of otters, with their slides and gambols, make them so likeable and engaging to humans. Minks, on the other hand, show no playfulness in their pursuit of fish, frogs, and other prey. Like their cousins the weasels, minks will kill more than they need to eat.

I realize that we humans should not judge animal species by our standards of sympathy and compassion, but I have gained no liking for the minks, even though they may be no more devastating to trout populations than otters. One incident comes to mind, when I saw a mother and three young otters coming busily down a brook, not missing any possible hiding place for a trout. When they spotted me standing at the head of a pool, they detoured around me for a short distance and entered the brook no more than ten yards below, providing a good view of their antics and industry to my wife Lila sitting on the bank. The fact that I still found trout in the section of stream they had just "fished" left no resentment for their depredation on the trout population.

East Branch of Fever Brook

KNOWN TO LOCAL FISHERMEN AS SHATTUCK BROOK, the East Branch of Fever Brook is also boggy and slow, interspersed with rapid stretches, some of them

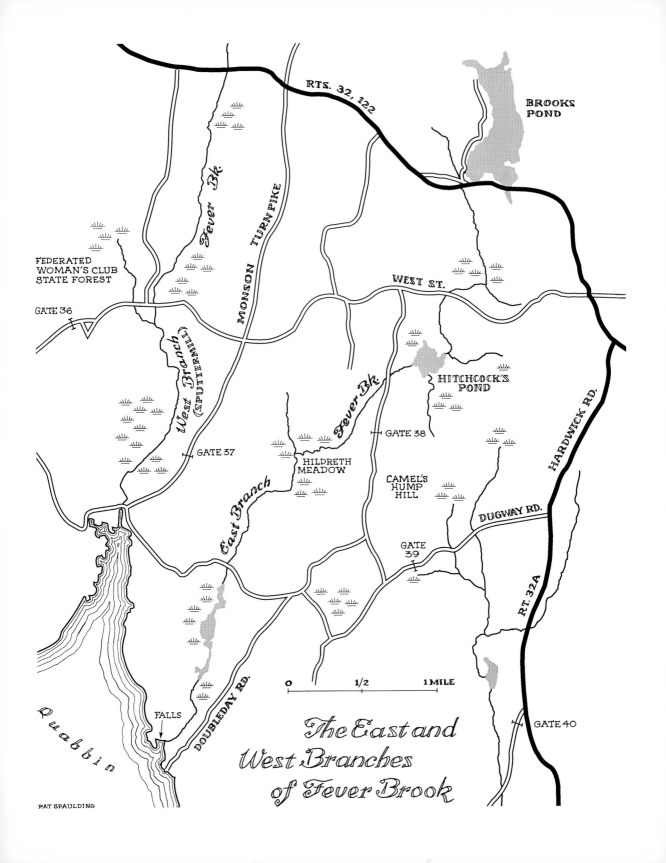

BROOKS POND

RTS. 32, 122

Fever Bk.

MONSON TURNPIKE

FEDERATED
WOMAN'S CLUB
STATE FOREST

GATE 36

WEST ST.

West Branch (SPUTTERMILL)

HITCHCOCK'S POND

Fever Bk.

GATE 38

HARDWICK RD.

GATE 37

East Branch

HILDRETH
MEADOW

CAMEL'S
HUMP
HILL

DUGWAY RD.

GATE 39

RT. 32A

0   1/2   1 MILE

Quabbin

DOUBLEDAY RD.

FALLS

GATE 40

The East and
West Branches
of Fever Brook

PAT SPAULDING

extensive, particularly the stretch from Camel's Hump Road to Hildreth Meadow. It flows from the southern end of Brooks Pond in Petersham in a southwesterly direction to its former junction with the West Branch of Fever. Much of the description of Sputtermill Brook also applies to Shattuck although the latter is a longer stream with a larger flow of water. Some of the beaver ponds on this brook are also extensive, and a once large population of wild, native brook trout has dwindled to a few fish that appear mainly in the months when the water is sufficiently cold to support their activity. It was also known as a stream where large trout lurked, but I have no information on the size or prevalence of these fish. The drop in elevation of this stream from Brooks Pond to its former confluence with the West Branch of Fever is three hundred feet over a distance of about five miles.

Very soon after the Quabbin area was opened to fishermen in 1946, I recall fishing the East Branch of Fever in the company of my father and Chet Baxter, who grew up in North Dana. Chet was confident the stream would have acquired a population of large brook trout during the years since the late Thirties when the Quabbin area was closed and the brook was fished very little if at all. He remembered it as a stream supporting a fairly good population of small trout, with an occasional fish of a pound or over in weight. After six or seven years of practically no fishing, we found it in the same state as far as trout population is concerned. The larger trout were no more numerous than previously. Even then, before the flooding of the stream by beavers, the extensive areas of slow water and muddy bottom prevented the generation of the large population of trout found in the colder waters of the West Branch of Swift River and the upper reaches of the Middle Branch. Today, with the very extensive beaver flowages on this stream, causing warming of the water, the trout have been driven to colder streams.

The forests and vegetation bordering the branches of Fever Brook are much the same as found along the streams on the west side of the Middle Branch and over the ridge along West Branch waters. There is a considerable amount of white pine in the adjacent forests, but somewhat less hemlock. There is also a greater prevalence of oak and other hardwoods, similarly to the lower stretches of the West and Middle Branches. The boggy meadows of the two branches of Fever Brook were well graced with the wild rose still found in bogs that have survived flooding by beavers or have recovered from the flooding.

Remains of stone dams exist just above and below Camel's Hump Road. The dam above the road flooded a sizable area once known as Hitchcock's Pond.

There was also a small dam just below the Hitchcock's Pond dam. Hitchcock's Pond is again a pond, impounded by beavers, but the remains of the dam below the road sit in a section of rapids. There was also a dam, and remains of a pond, just above the road that crosses the brook several miles below, running from Hell Huddle to the Monson Turnpike. I believe the stream was also dammed at one time above the falls where it presently drops into the reservoir.

I recall one beautiful afternoon in May, before Hitchcock's Pond was re-flooded by beavers. The brook flowed deep through walls of tall grass, and trout had gathered in numbers. It was possible to get out a fairly long cast, and I was having excellent luck catching "eating size" trout. While retrieving one fish, I looked up from my concentration on the trout and found a deer watching me from the other bank. I had heard that deer are curious, a contention that was amply proved. He walked up to the edge of the bank and stayed to watch me retrieve another trout. Unconcerned and unafraid, the deer then wandered slowly away.

Below the rapids running from Camel's Hump Road, Hildreth Meadow was another area of slow water and high grass, but I never happened to find any appreciable accumulation of trout there. I did find a good bunch of trout in a small brook running into the meadow where someone had erected a small cement dam, however. Since then, this brook, although quite small, has cut away the bank adjacent to the dam, and that diminutive pond no longer provides a deep, cold water resting place for the trout. Hildreth Meadow is again a beaver flowage, and trout have pretty well disappeared from this section of the stream. Nevertheless, it provides excellent habitat for waterfowl and other wildlife.

Sputtermill Brook, the west branch of Fever Brook

A beaver pond on Tyre Brook, a Middle Branch tributary

Keystone Bridge near Daniel Shays Highway on Middle Branch

High water on the East Branch

The East Branch

AT HIGHER ELEVATION THAN MOST OF THE WEST AND MIDDLE BRANCHES, the trout waters of the East Branch have escaped inundation by the Quabbin Reservoir. Before Quabbin was created, trout water on the East Branch existed mainly above Pottapaug Pond in Dana. Most of it is still above the high water mark and survives as fishable. Trout were found below Pottapaug, but usually during the high water of the spring or fall. Because of the greater elevation of its area of trout breeding and its carrying capacity, the East Branch has a different character than the West and Middle branches. The East Branch is primarily a rocky stream strewn with boulders. A gravel bottom does not appear until below Nichewaug, so the stream must also have escaped the prolonged flooding by glacial retreat that evidently took place on the West and Middle branches.

There are two distinct East Branch sections. The upper end, known as Popple Camp Brook, is slow and boggy. Below, the remainder of the stream is fast with a rocky bottom. Popple Camp consists of a series of grassy, boggy "meadows" separated by short sections of somewhat faster water. The upper fishable stretch in Popple Camp includes Upper Meadow and Dunn Meadow, separated by a short stretch of water flowing fast through a wooded area. Dunn Meadow held large numbers of trout in the early part of the season. In the warm months of July and August, however, most trout had migrated to the cooler waters of the Upper Meadow and the wooded stretches above and below it.

Yet another extensive boggy stretch flows down from Popple Camp Road. It too is populated with trout during the months of colder water. Below the bog, the stream starts its rocky course to Pottapaug. The bottom of Popple Camp Brook is generally sand or gravel overlaid in places with mud. East Branch water does not share the gin-like clarity of the West or Middle branches. Instead, at times, it has an orange tint. Some attribute East Branch coloration to the extraction of decaying vegetation in the boggy upper section of the stream. However, I have seen numerous streams in upper New Hampshire, Maine, Nova Scotia, and Newfoundland that originated in bogs and did not have an orange coloration. I believe it is more likely due to deposits of minerals containing iron in the upper areas of the watershed. In some sections of Popple Camp the bottom has a more reddish tinge, especially pronounced in a tributary appropriately named Red Brook that enters the Upper Meadow.

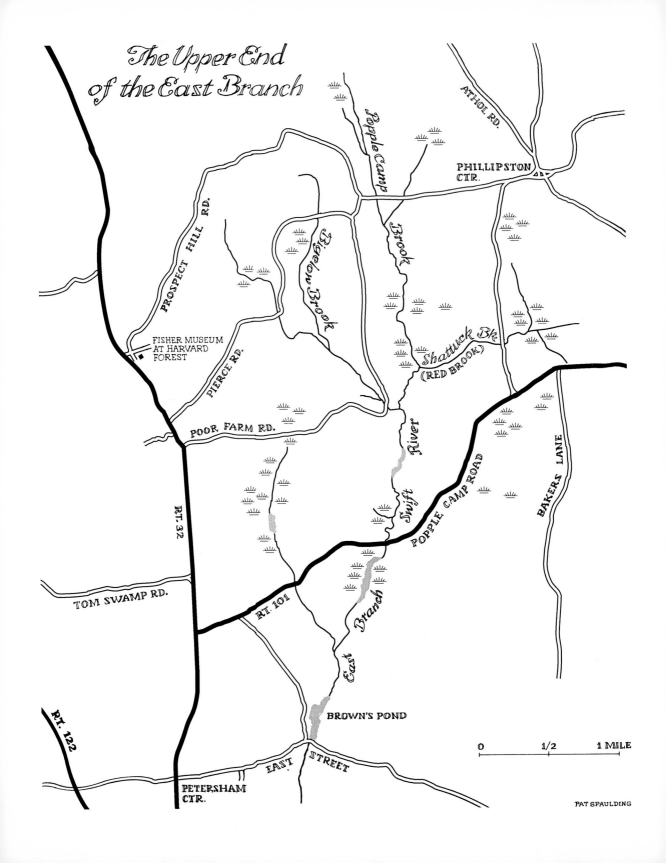

The Upper End of the East Branch

Below the boggy meadows of Popple Camp, the East Branch runs through a heavily forested terrain with many of the same plant and tree species observed along the West and Middle branches. The Canada mayflower appears in extensive colonies in the woods, and since I fish the East Branch during the spring, I am more aware of mayflower distribution along the East Branch than elsewhere. White pine and hemlock are prevalent, with a good population of oaks and birches. Maples become more prevalent in the broader flood plain below Nichewaug where the stream has more grassy areas, probably a result of former beaver flowages.

Since the return of beavers to the watershed, many former ponds have been rebuilt. Small natural diversions in the flood plain of the East Branch have also become sizable beaver ponds. While such diversions or overflow channels do not normally hold more than fingerling trout, a pond built on such a site by beavers soon has a sizable population of fairly large trout. The water chemistry resulting from the flooding is evidently attractive to the trout, since unflooded channels do not support numbers of mature fish. The changing aspect caused by beavers in streams of the Swift River watershed therefore gives to trout fishing an element of searching for fresh beaver ponds conducive to trout. After the ponds have remained for several years, however, the water chemistry undergoes a further change possibly due to acidity. As the water becomes less desirable to the trout, they leave the ponds. Rough warm water species may remain, however.

One section of the East Branch where beavers have become more or less permanent residents is found below Brown's Pond. Evidence of their former existence is found in the grassy, brushy meadows that existed prior to their return. The area at the head of Connor's Pond is another section frequented by beavers. The man-made ponds on the East Branch, Brown's, and Connor's ponds, are still in existence. A sizable millpond was formerly just below the bridge on the road leading east from Nichewaug. The stone foundations of a mill are still in evidence, but the remains of the wooden dam below disappeared sometime in the late 1940s. Large colonies of Solomon's seal grow on nearby steep banks. Another dam was sited at Nichewaug, as shown on the geologic survey map of 1894, and a sizable section of it may still be seen today. There is at that site an appreciable drop in the stream over a succession of cascades that have a wild and formidable aspect in a spate.

The Dunn Meadow of Popple Camp was flooded in 1922 and provided local fishermen with better than average-sized trout during that season. It may have undergone changes similar to those of beaver ponds today, creating attractive conditions. The brook, however, found a way around the cement dams during the following winter, and the pond was not restored. The trunks of flooded trees remained for years, giving a wild touch to the meadow not found on other streams of the area. Remains of dead trees are now seen on most brooks of the watershed since beavers have returned to establish their ponds, which remain for a time.

For most of its course, the East Branch runs through a rather narrow valley with steep hillsides. Most of the valley was never cultivated. The forests along the East Branch are therefore ancient in many sections. Because of the narrowness of the valley and the height of the adjacent hills, many of the forests escaped destruction during the 1938 hurricane. Unfortunately, the impressive stand of pine and hemlock in Harvard Forest above Connor's Pond did not escape. The forest has since been allowed to regenerate naturally, and it is interesting to follow the succession of trees and plants in the area that was most affected by the winds. There is still a magnificent forest above the blown down area, and the valley holds some extremely large black cherry trees, for this region at least, along with pine, hemlock, and oak.

The woods below Connor's Pond are also in a remarkable state of preservation and look much the same today as they must have when the first English settlers arrived. Huge pines and hemlocks grow along the banks, providing sufficient shade to promote the growth of mosses and ferns instead of woody species. A very open character to the immediate environment of the brook adds an element of great beauty. The exceptionally large and ancient conifers in many locations grow quite close together and seem to violate some of the present tenets of forestry that large trees should be well-spaced. In many places, the banks are shelving rock ledges, overhung with hemlock. The flanking pools are of mouthwatering beauty, at least to fishermen. The East Branch gives an aspect of great antiquity with exposed ancient rocks and large conifers, as well as huge logs tumbling down steep banks. It is fortunate the woods along this stream have been so well preserved and that so much of it escaped inundation. This is particularly true because of the great beauty and interest of the area.

The unspoiled section of the stream below Connor's Pond was owned by the Choate family during the late 1800s and early 1900s. In order to keep hunters and fishermen out of his domain, the Choate who controlled the land along the stream in that era moved a family of Indians from Maine to live on and

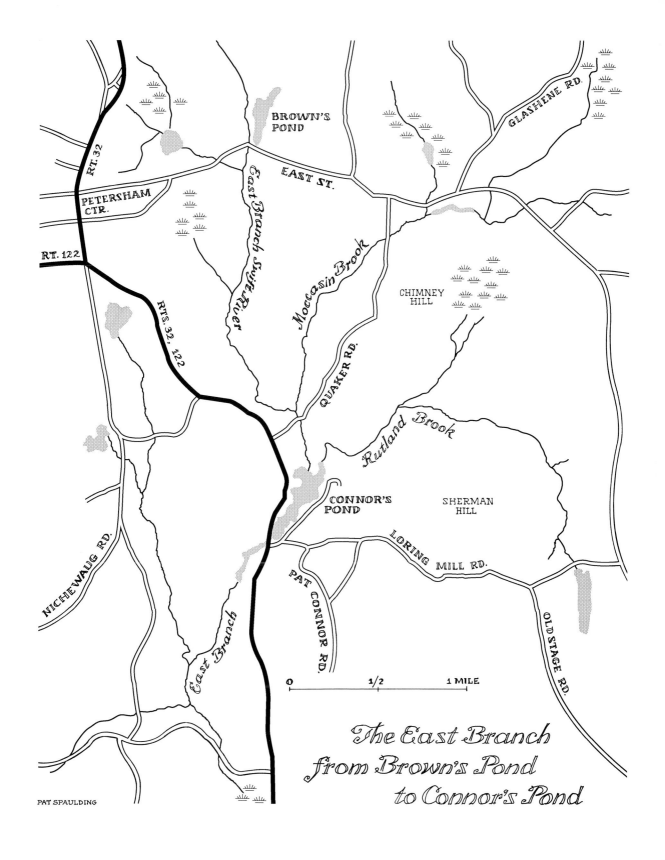

The East Branch
from Brown's Pond
to Connor's Pond

patrol the property. Few if any local sportsmen who trespassed in the woods were able to escape the detection of the Indians. For a relatively long period, the section of stream was unfished, with the exception of an occasional visit by Mr. Choate and friends. My first acquaintance with the primitive Choate stretch came in the 1940s, some time after the disappearance of the Indian family. The brook at that time, a period when there were few local fishermen because of World War II, was well populated with native brook trout, generally running from eight to twelve inches, with occasional specimens up to fifteen inches.

Another aspect of trout fishing on the East Branch, particularly below Connor's Pond, differs from fishing on the West and Middle Branches. On the East Branch, water warms during the summer months. From roughly the middle of June to the middle of August, brook trout are not to be seen in this stream. They either find spring-fed spots or remain dormant in the warm water for a couple of months. In either case, they reappear in late August and resume feeding. If they do congregate in colder, spring-fed spots, as found in some of the wilderness streams of New Hampshire, Maine, or the Maritime Provinces of Canada, I have never been able to locate them. Some fishermen claim they have caught brown and rainbow trout in this stretch of the stream during the summer, but in my experience they have not been found.

Another puzzling aspect of the East Branch is the great variation from year to year in the native brook trout population of the stream. In some years, the more favorable stretches hold large numbers of native trout, whereas in others, the native trout are relatively scarce. It is probably due to the success of breeding in a given year two or three years prior to the year of low population that may result from excessively high water at the time the fry hatch in late winter. High water could wash out gravelled spots where fertilized eggs were buried or prevent the fry from reaching a spot safe from the current after hatching. In any case, the East Branch has much less of the gravelled bottom needed for egg survival than either the West or Middle Branch, but it is apparently sufficient to provide relatively large numbers of fish in favorable years. The uneven trout population is countered to some extent by the state's trout stocking program. It generally provides a good number of trout in the ten- to fifteen-inch range. They weigh between about a half pound and a pound and a quarter. The East Branch has a drop in elevation of about six hundred fifty feet over a distance of about ten miles from its source in the swamps of Phillipston to Pottapaug Pond.

East Branch Tributaries

NONE OF THE FEEDER STREAMS OF THE EAST BRANCH is large enough to be considered fishable trout water, at least from the point of view of the fly fisherman. Moccasin Brook may be an exception, affording a few pools in its downhill course to the East Branch where the worm fisherman can maneuver. A small pond exists in the upper reaches of Moccasin barely large enough to allow the fly caster an opportunity to raise a mature trout or two. Red Brook flowing into the Upper Meadow of Popple Camp, was also fished by the bait fishermen earlier in the century. It was a favorite of Arthur Starrett of Athol. Another brook large enough for the bait fisherman to maneuver is Carter Brook, particularly in the lower end before its junction with the East Branch just below Nichewaug. The pool on the main stream where this brook enters over a diminutive waterfall is breathtaking, overhung with hemlock and supporting a rich cover of moss and ferns on the banks. It has been a most favorable location for trout to gather in the past, but it was partially spoiled when tractors used the rapids at the head of the pool as a crossing place during a logging operation. The stream is gradually erasing the indignity, however.

A small brook that joins the main stream at the westward bend in the Choate stretch is again too small to be considered fishable, but it has a pond in the upper end that harbors trout. Recently, beavers have enlarged the pond, and the trout population has fluctuated in accordance with the usual sequence of events in a beaver pond. Rutland Brook and another very small, evidently unnamed brook entering the river just above Pottapaug also have beaver ponds that hold trout.

Silver Brook is another tributary large enough to allow a bait fisherman room to operate in places, but Carter Pond, a sizable pond upstream, is better. Carter Pond was originally controlled and kept for the use of a private club, most of whose members were from the Boston area. Club members hired a caretaker to live at the pond and keep other fishermen out. The man they hired was George Sutherland from Athol, a businessman of thirty-seven who had been told by his physician he had only two years to live. George decided to leave his family and spend his remaining two years leading a solitary life at Carter Pond.

It must have been curative because, at the time I talked with him in 1960, George was over ninety. His life at Carter Pond was not just one of enjoying solitude. He built a fish hatchery and, experimenting over the years, found the conditions of water flow and temperature best suited to give a large yield of fry from the eggs laid and fertilized by "his" trout. He managed to get the trout from the pond into the hatchery by letting the water out each fall just prior to the time of spawning. Spawning generally occurred during the early part of December on a dark, stormy day, according to George. I have observed trout spawning in local streams somewhat earlier in the fall, but this is probably due to the colder waters of the brooks in comparison to the warmer pond water for George's trout. I understand that George's methods and hatchery pools became known, and officials from states in the process of setting up trout hatcheries benefited by the knowledge of the subject he had gained.

The three branches of Swift River and their valleys were quite different in appearance. The East Branch, with the exception of the upper end, or Popple Camp Brook, is a fast, rocky stream traversing a rather narrow valley with often steep banks. The Middle Branch below the Toad Hollow meadows was a slow stream in a much wider valley which below Millington was unusually flat for New England. The West Branch valley below Dickeyville was intermediate in size between valleys of the East and Middle Branch. Also, the East Branch had a rocky bed, and at times, orange-tinted water. The Middle Branch had a mud bottom in many locations, and sandy bottom in others. The West Branch had mainly a sand or gravel bottom below the cobble stones in the upper reaches. Greater differences in stream type can be found in the tributaries, making the whole watershed one of great diversity in stream type and surroundings. With the continual creation of beaver ponds, it is clear that a considerable variety in the trout habitat is characteristic of this region, and gives the trout enthusiast a wealth of waters to enjoy.

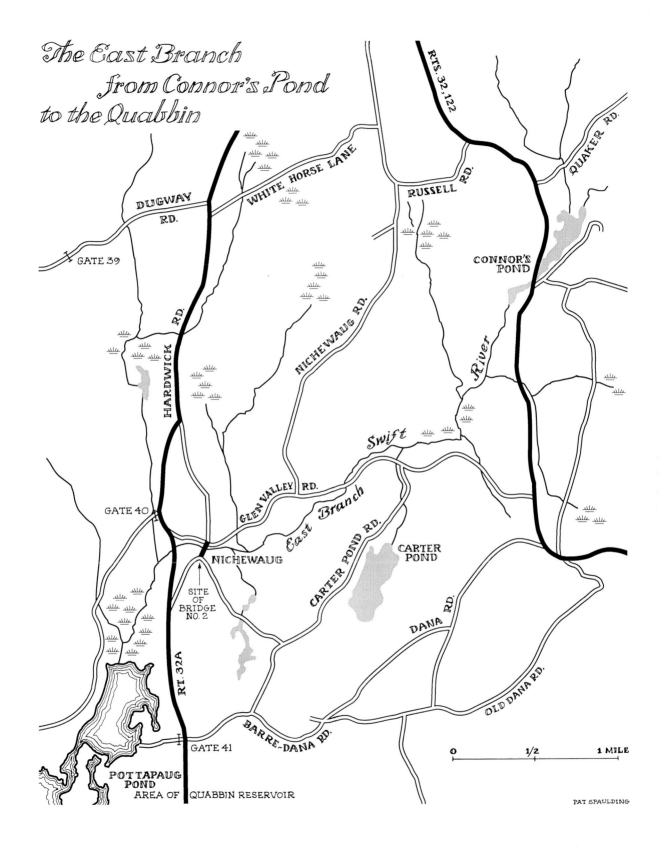

The East Branch from Connor's Pond to the Quabbin

RTS. 32,122

QUAKER RD.

WHITE HORSE LANE

RUSSELL RD.

DUGWAY RD.

CONNOR'S POND

GATE 39

HARDWICK RD.

NICHEWAUG RD.

River

Swift

GATE 40

GLEN VALLEY RD.

East Branch

CARTER POND RD.

CARTER POND

NICHEWAUG

SITE OF BRIDGE NO. 2

DANA RD.

RT. 32A

OLD DANA RD.

BARRE~DANA RD.

GATE 41

POTTAPAUG POND

AREA OF QUABBIN RESERVOIR

0   1/2   1 MILE

PAT SPAULDING

Crossing an island to fish near Nichewaug

Fishing a pool on the East Branch

Casting a run on the East Branch

Netting a brookie

Bill Foye examines a delectable little native

Trout Fishing In Smaller Streams

THE TROUT FISHING HABITS OF OUR FATHERS AND GRANDFATHERS, at least in the rather small but wonderfully varied area of the sources of Swift River, differed markedly from those of the more avid trout fishermen of today. Today's trout enthusiasts prefer larger waters and larger trout. While it has been pleasurable for me to fish both large and small streams, I find my preference is for small brooks where casting is difficult and the size of trout caught is small. For many reasons, fishing on small brooks gives a satisfaction not matched on larger streams. There is the necessity for an accurately cast fly, often within a few inches, to interest a trout spied in an almost inaccessible spot. There is also the necessity for getting the trout in only a cast or two, before the fly is hung in the brush or on a log. A cast just a bit too heavy scares the fish. The closer proximity of vegetation—ferns, flowering plants, and trees—provides a greater feeling of mingling with nature. I like to feel that I am part of the environment and not an intruder trespassing on the domain of the trout. Historical aspects of the streams and the presence of former dams and millponds add to the interest of trout fishing in this area. Finally, it is intriguing to have the ability to locate the exact spot where an incident of importance, at least to a trout enthusiast, took place years ago. All such attributes of small stream fishing give more meaning than the pursuit of trophy size trout in a much less exacting setting. There is the realization of fitting into the "scheme of things," to use the words of Frost.

Difficulties experienced while fishing small trout streams in heavily forested, often brushy surroundings may make it seem not worth the effort to some. I find, however, that the difficulties and obstacles provide much of the satisfaction of the actual art of fly fishing. The proximity of vegetation and wildlife—and often of the trout themselves—also provides an element of wildness. There is a sense of entering the realm of another species of life and of being able to discern its impulses, fears, and habits. While fishing a small brook, I have a feeling of existing for a short time on an equal footing with these creatures. It provides a "life apart" not experienced in many other types of fishing.

Difficult casting and keeping the fly from being hung in vegetation are not the only obstacles that give the pursuit of small trout its zest and interest. The approach to the pools also provides challenge. In order to catch trout in any waters they inhabit, the fish must not be disturbed by any unnatural motion of branch, bank, shadow, or, of course, sight of a fisherman. An extremely cautious approach must be made to the pool to be cast. Often a little planning is in order as to the best location, so the fisherman will be visible to the smallest or least productive part of the pool. The fisherman may need to assume an awkward posture for some time, at least until satisfied that the fly has been presented in a "natural" manner to the spots where the trout are most likely to lie. In covering several miles of stream over rocks and logs, perhaps through patches of mountain laurel, there is a good amount of exercise necessary for three or four hours' fishing. Further exercise is sometimes provided by climbing trees to retrieve "hung" flies, an endeavor fraught with the possibility of the tree or branch breaking to plunge the fisherman into the stream. My young son found such prospects more intriguing than the fishing.

Another hazard of trout fishing more prevalent in smaller streams is the sometimes hidden presence of underwater branches, logs, and water plants. If the fisherman has been able to keep the fly from hooking such natural parts of the trout's habitat and defenses, the trout, once hooked, will attempt to use them in escape attempts by wrapping the line around them or hooking the hook into them. Trout will also attempt to wrap the line or leader around rocks. With a direct pull on the line and without the cushioning effect of the rod, a trout may be able to tear its mouth off the hook relatively easily because of the very small size of hooks used in artificial flies. A trout with line thus wrapped may also break the leader. Because leaders are fine enough at a two or three pound test to escape the detection of the trout in its usually fast rise to the fly, they are quite easy to break with a direct pull. I once hooked a brown trout of about a pound and a half in a small brush-lined stream with a sand bottom. It managed to wrap the line around underwater branches four or five times before I was able to get it into the net. Because the water that day was exceptionally high, I had used stronger leader than usual, and the trout was unable to break it. However, each time I managed to free the line from a tangle, the trout immediately swam downstream with the current. It then gained a little slack line by swimming back upstream a short distance where it was able to wrap the line around another alder branch. The process repeated itself at least four times and through as many pools before the trout was finally netted. Back at the car, I was showing the trout to Otis Gray, my fishing partner of about thirty years, when a car screeched to a halt. The driver got out, took a look at the fish, and remarked that such a large trout couldn't possibly have come out of a brook so small.

I recall many instances of catching much smaller trout in spots almost inaccessible, at least to fly casting. The occasions were equally memorable. One in particular, on a bright July evening, took place where the brook ran under a pile of logs and branches left by high water—an obvious spot for sheltering trout. A fly fisherman ahead of me had cast the open water above the log pile and had seen no sign of fish. With one well placed cast just an inch or two short of the logs, I raised and landed a beautiful native trout of about three-quarters of a pound.

I remember landing a much smaller brookie in a fast spot where it was necessary to make a loop cast behind a branch overhanging the center of the pool. The trout, of course, was on the other side of the branch. The first cast looped the fly upstream behind the branch and succeeded in taking the trout; with fast action with the rod, I was able to get the trout below the branch before it was able to get hung up in it. I remember a similar incident when there were only about two to three feet of fast, open water where the fly could be presented above a stick lying across the pool. It required a cast at the "head" of the stretch overhung with grass and getting the fly off the water before it got lodged on the stick. Because of the speed of the current, the fly was in view of the trout for no more than a second. It was sufficient, however, and the trout rose and was hooked. I was able to lift it out while it was still at the surface. Otherwise, the trout would have gotten under the stick and probably succeeded in leaving the hook in it.

For parents attempting to interest their children in the gentle art of trout fishing, more open streams with fewer natural hazards provide a more satisfactory, less frustrating setting than the little brooks. After several attempts on reasonably open streams with my son Owen, I took him to a stream with no underbrush at all and fast, rocky pools. His first trout was caught under a ledge just below a four- or five-foot falls. He followed instructions perfectly, got out on the ledge without scaring the trout, and lowered a worm over the side. A nine- or ten-inch trout took it immediately, and Owen landed it after a short struggle. I believe his excitement matched my satisfaction. In any case, it was an important event in a family for whom he is the fourth generation to fish streams of western Massachusetts.

As a boy, I also much preferred the more open, rocky, downhill streams where chances of having the hook hung in some irretrievable spot were much less than in the streams I now find challenging. In those days, I fished with other boys: Pete Kimball, Doug Roth, Bud Thompson, Jackie Rist, Don Walton. Our huge dog Fritz, part German shepherd and part St. Bernard, was always with us. He soon learned he was not supposed to get into the water ahead of us and scare the trout. His usual tactic was to go down the bank first and find a comfortable place with good visibility, lie down, and wait for us to catch up. Fritz thus found a much more acceptable practice for waiting over trout not already scared than I later experienced with a young English setter named Piney Woods. On seeing a trout fighting on the end of the line, Piney would go in after it, often ending with the hook somewhere on himself.

I found another apologist for fishing smaller streams in Muriel Foster, an English woman who fished Scotland in the early part of the century, most often in lochs and larger rivers. In *Muriel Foster's Fishing Diary*, published in 1980 by The Viking Press in New York, is a poem expressing her delight in fishing smaller trout waters:

> *Not at once of Test and Itchen*
> *Sing I, nor of Kennet's state*
> *Whence my fario come to kitchen*
> *Salmon-pink and grampus-great,*
> *But, though Berkshire's bulrush quivers,*
> *But, though Hampshire's king cups out,*
> *First I'll sing of little rivers*
> *And of very little trout.*
>
> *Little trout whose claims do beckon*
> *So insistently and sound,*
> *Little trout whose bulk we reckon*
> *Six or seven to the pound—*
> *These I'll sing, to these beholden,*
> *These long since a song did earn,*
> *Crimson-spotted, plump and golden,*
> *Flung a-kicking from the burn.*

Leaping down the brown hill's shoulder
Trailed of birk and mountain ash,
Beat upon by granite boulder,
Little waters hop and splash;
Pied by snows of last December,
Bens above the May days flout
Ah! That's how you'll best remember
Little rivers, little trout!

Grease your brogues with dreamland tallow,
Forth with me and fish like kings,
And by pot and swirling shallow
Fill a creel with fingerlings,
Where our noses first got blistered,
Where our greenhearts first went "swish,"
Where the paws of boyhood glistered
With the scales of little fish.

Those were days, you say? Why then it
Scarce is odd if thus I wink,
'Ere we walk by lovely Kennet.
'Ere we follow Itchen's brink,
Where the Berkshire bulrush quivers,
Where the Hampshire king cups out,
Wink with love at little rivers,
And at very little trout.

— 1917

April 15 - Moss Village   9

"   17 - Canada & Swift R.   12

"   19 - Dickeys   "   "   4

"   22 - Village   "   "   16

"   24 - Mill & Sangor   0

"   25 - Tuffy   0

"   26 - Poplar Camp   0

"   29 - Village & Type   2

May 6 - Murdock Pond   3

"   7 - Brown Brook   1

"   8 - Murdock Pond   1

"   9 - Greeley   0

"   11 - Moosehorn   12

"   13 - Swift R.   18

"   16 - "   "   6

"   18 - "   "   5

"   20 - Cranberry Meadow   5

"   22 - Poplar Camp   0

A page from Owen Foye's 1917 trout-fishing record

Weather, Rainfall, Acid Rain

WEATHER AND RAINFALL ARE THE MOST CRITICAL FACTORS IN THE MAINTENANCE of a sufficient supply of cold, running water necessary for the survival of trout. The periods of drought experienced in the Thirties and to a lesser extent in the mid-Sixties did not appear to affect the trout population to any appreciable degree in the area of the upper Swift River watershed. Also, the warming trend of the Eighties has not yet had a noticeable effect on the native trout populations of this area. The presence of beaver ponds to provide depth and cover with the constant flow of cold water from springs has kept the streams in relatively good condition. During periods of low water, usually in late summer, I have found trout under rocks in small brooks with a barely visible flow of water. It seems hardly possible that fish could survive under such circumstances, but the evidence is that they do—as long as the brook does not dry up completely, of course. While fishing in the fall, I have noticed numerous trout that did not appear to have added any weight over the summer months. They were probably trapped in one of the small tributaries they went up in the spring to start their heavy feeding for the year and were probably unable to get downstream again before the water dropped. It is fortunate there is still adequate feed in the fall months to sustain them through the winter.

It is apparent fish can survive rather extreme changes in brook flow, but variations in the weather and resulting amount of rainfall have much to do with the population of mature trout from year to year. Perhaps flood conditions during the winter or early spring, which might alter the gravel beds holding developing embryos, have the greatest effect on the population of mature trout showing up several years later. I have not been able to observe a connection between the resulting hatch and the exceptionally high water in the winter and early spring, however. The fry are so tiny they are not easily observed until at least a year later. It is also not possible to separate the results of such flood conditions on hatching trout from other factors such as summer drought, natural predation, fishing pressure, or the occasional tour of a family of otters up one of the brooks. The fact that native trout populations fluctuate is probably best recorded in the fishing success of a given stream from year to year, at least by those with enough scientific interest or long range outlook to keep records of trout caught.

I was struck by fluctuation in fishing success while reading Muriel Foster's delightful fishing diary. She kept records of her catch of trout during the Teens and Twenties, at a time when fewer people were fishing. One would assume the trout population was regulated mainly by conditions of weather that affected hatching and survival of the fry, but not by stocking. I was more startled when I compared her records with those of my father during the same period. While the parallelism is not exact, his years of high catches in some cases were the same as hers, and some of the years of low catches were the same for both. If the weather patterns of New England and Scotland are similar, then this coincidence can be explained. A study of total precipitation in Massachusetts and northern Scotland would probably not provide the explanation, since it would not include the periods of drought or flooding that occurred. In corresponding with my good friend Professor John Midgley of Glasgow for a number of years, however, I have been able to ascertain that their wet and dry years generally correspond with our own. The parallelism between the fishing success of Muriel Foster and Owen H. Foye is shown in Table I. Both were good anglers, and stocking was not significant in those days. High averages for both are seen for 1917, 1927, and 1930. Low averages for both occurred in 1925. Fair agreement (0.5 difference in averages) is found in 1923 and 1926. There is a distinct lack of agreement in 1924, 1928, and 1929, although in 1929, my father fished only during the early season. The summer months were taken up in the auction of the Foye jewelry business; my father could foresee the coming economic depression and sold the business.

The gradual increase in the acidity of precipitation as well as dry deposition of acids over the past forty years has added another element of far greater destructive potential to the health and survival of trout and the whole ecological system on which they depend. It is already well recorded that a sizable percentage of the lakes of the Adirondack region as well as lakes and streams of eastern Canada, having low buffering capacity for acid, have lost the ability to support aquatic life. The buffering capacity of the soil and minerals of central and western Massachusetts is somewhat greater, but in time can be overcome if the amount of acid increases or even continues at its present level. Some areas of Massachusetts are already nearing their limit for buffering further additions of acid. The Miller's River watershed, just to the north and east of the Swift River watershed, is apparently one such area. Trout populations in the tributaries of the Miller's have declined to a much greater extent than in those of the Swift River watershed.

Table I

Trout Fishing Records of Owen H. Foye, Massachusetts, and Muriel Foster, Scotland

	Owen H. Foye		Muriel Foster	
Year	Total Trout	Trout Per Trip	Total Trout	Trout Per Trip
1917	401	7.3	222	7.0
1923	235	4.9	64	4.3
1924	173	3.8	120	4.8
1925	130	3.7	105	3.3
1926	101	3.5	152	4.1
1927	216	5.1	171	5.0
1928	257	6.3	110	3.8
1929	107	5.4	70	3.0
1930	69	5.3	83	4.9

The acid deposition responsible for the deleterious and ultimately lethal effect on aquatic life, along with terrestrial effects not yet fully recognized, comes from two major sources: coal burning power plants and the automobile. The first liberates sulphur oxides that are converted to sulfuric acid in the atmosphere. The second liberates nitrogen oxides that are converted to nitric and related acids. The combination of their effluents amounts to millions of tons of acids dumped on the northeastern part of the United States and eastern part of Canada each year. Other areas of the country are also experiencing the effect in various degrees. The question has been raised regarding the burning of coal for both industrial and home use in the late 1800s and 1900s up until the Forties, and why it did not produce an acidic threat then. Coal burning in those days did not include the removal of ash from the smoke and flue gases, and the ash provides roughly an equivalent amount of alkali which neutralizes the acid. With the removal of the alkaline ash, and the construction of the very tall smoke stacks of the power plants today, relatively pure sulfur oxides are liberated and able to travel with the prevailing winds to be deposited as acid hundreds of miles away. As for the automobile, the threat from exhaust of both acid and ozone producing gases did not become serious until post-World War II prosperity put a huge number of cars on the road. The technology already exists to neutralize a considerable amount of such acidic effluents, but the major factor against their adoption, of course, has been the cost. The cost of losing not only trout producing but also safe drinking water is far greater and of a longer lasting effect. The argument is raised that liming of our drinking water, or other ways of neutralizing the acid, can be used to bring the pH back to neutral. These methods, however, do not remove the small amounts of highly toxic mineral elements that are leached from the soil and minerals of the watersheds and accumulate in the lakes and reservoirs. Such toxic minerals, among them mercury and aluminum, also accumulate in the tissues of fish—and also in the tissues of humans if they drink the water over extended periods. Signs put up by the Division of Fisheries and Wildlife have already appeared to warn of the danger of eating too many fish from several streams and lakes including the Quabbin Reservoir. The effect on the human population using these waters as drinking water has yet to be recognized, but eventually toxic levels in humans could result unless methods are put in place to remove these elements. Such methods would be far more costly than those required to keep the acids out of the environment in the first place by limiting both sulfur and nitrogen emissions.

The amount of acidity in water is due to the hydrogen ion concentration. Measurement of hydrogen ion concentration is done by pH meters. The pH scale for water runs from 0 to 14, with extremely strong acids having negative numbers. pH units are logarithmic so a difference of one pH unit is a ten-fold difference in acidity. A pH of 7 indicates neutrality, or an even balance between acidic and alkaline functions. Above a pH of 7, the water is alkaline. Below 7, it is acidic. Aquatic life starts dying below a pH of 5, if sustained for an appreciable period. The pH of individual rainstorms has been recorded in the New England area as low as 3, which is 10,000 times more acidic than neutral water. Soils and minerals, such as limestone, containing calcium or magnesium have the ability to neutralize acidity. This feature is called a buffering capacity. There is some limestone in the Swift River watershed, but it is not one of the more prevalent minerals.

Although some limitation of sulfur and nitrogen emissions has been accomplished, much more needs to be achieved. The effects of the acid on soils and minerals are cumulative in releasing and mobilizing toxic metals. There is more topsoil in central New England than farther north in Canada, where the

Laurentian Shield north of Montreal is scarcely covered with soil. Lakes and rivers are seriously damaged there. A greater buffering effect on acid is available in central New England. Once the acid and toxic metals it liberates are in a body of water like the Quabbin Reservoir, where buffering capacity is limited, the acidity will continue to increase as long as present levels of sulfur and nitrogen emissions are maintained. Bacteria probably play a role in controlling acidity through their ability to decompose organic matter, but I have seen no published studies on this aspect of acid control. The already dead lakes of the Adirondacks, eastern Canada, and northern Europe are evidence that the buffering capacities of those areas have been overcome. Once dead, the lakes cannot be restored to their former balance of living species.

Because of a serious concern for the effects of the increasing acidity of the trout waters as well as our drinking water, I started measuring the pH of the Swift River branches and tributaries several years ago. A portable pH meter became a standard part of my trout fishing gear, now more commonly used to ascertain trout numbers than to provide fish for the table. As a professor of chemistry having access to laboratories where the pH meter could be checked periodically against standard buffer solutions, I believe my measurements are accurate to within a tenth of a pH unit.

Results of these measurements are shown in Table II. pH measurements over a three-year period, 1987 to 1989, on these streams revealed a number of interesting, as well as disturbing, developments. First, there is a gradual increase in acidity of the tributaries at the very upper ends of the streams. The upper waters of the West Branch, in particular, have become dangerously close to the level, below a pH of 5.0, at which trout and other aquatic organisms cannot survive. As measurements are made further down these streams, the pH gradually increases. Apparently, the seepage from springs and underground water table, where the buffering ability of the limestone in the ridges comes into play, is providing water on the alkaline side of neutrality. Some of the small brooks that are mainly spring fed, such as Village Brook, run on the alkaline side, that is, over a pH of 7.0. There are still trout surviving in the upper waters of the West Branch, but nowhere near their former numbers. There is a decided absence of small trout in the upper stretches, however, so the trout still found there probably have migrated from downstream.

A second observation, related to the buffering capacity of the watershed soil and minerals is the rapidity with which the pH returns to its "normal" or presently existing level following a rainstorm. The pH undergoes a definite drop following an appreciable amount of rain during the summer and fall, but regains its former level within a day or two, depending on the amount of rainfall and its acidity. During the early spring, however, with the combined effects of acid precipitation and runoff from melting snow, also quite acidic, the streams remain acidic for a much more extended period of time, again depending on conditions. It is most unfortunate that this is the time when the fish eggs are hatching, with the fry entering an acidic environment. Up to the present, the trout hatches of the Swift River watershed have been able to survive such conditions, but each year I wonder whether the last hatch of native trout might already have taken place.

Many of the tributaries of the three branches of Swift River originate in bogs which are naturally acidic. This no doubt accounts, in part, for the acidic nature of the very upper ends of these brooks. The fact that the brooks farther downstream become closer to neutral or even alkaline conditions might offer hope that the trout populations can survive in them. However, large numbers of the fingerlings spend their first year in these upper reaches (or did formerly) and an increase in acidity of only half a pH unit could wipe out a generation of trout. And, if not corrected, such an increase could end the ability of the stream to support the survival of trout.

While there is still the realization that the amount of acid raining down on our environment has not yet killed the waters of the Swift River, there is also the benumbing realization that unless the amount of acid-producing gases entering the atmosphere is cut substantially, the native trout population, as well as all other aquatic life, could come to an end in a foreseeable period of time. Should this happen, our worry of the toxic effects of the water supply would be transferred to the human population dependent on these same waters.

Table II

pH Averages (May-August)

Stream	1987	1988	1989
West Branch	7.4	7.3	7.5
Village	8.1	8.0	7.8
Tyre	7.3	7.5	7.5
Moosehorn	7.4	7.1	7.0
Cadwick	6.4	6.5	6.7
Dickey		7.5	7.6
East Branch		6.5	7.3
Middle Branch		7.8	7.6

pH Readings at four locations along Canada Brook (August, 1987)

Below Cranberry Meadow (1/4 mile)	1 mile below	1 mile above Cooleyville	At Cooleyville
5.7	5.8	6.7	7.3

pH Readings at four locations on the upper West Branch (July, 1988)

1 mile above Cooleyville	1/2 mile above Cooleyville	At Cooleyville	1 mile below Cooleyville
5.3	5.5	6.9	7.3

ph Readings within 24 hours after rain

	1987	
	July	Average
West Branch at Cooleyville	6.0	7.4
Village Brook at Cooleyville	7.3	8.1
Canada Brook at Cooleyville	6.3	7.3

ph Readings, before/during snow runoff

	1990	
	January 1	March 17
West Branch at Daniel Shays Highway	7.3	6.4
West Branch at Shutesbury Road	6.9	5.2
Canada Brook at Shutesbury Road	7.0	5.4
Village Brook, Cooleyville	7.4	6.4
Tyre Brook, Paige Farm	7.1	6.4

Appendix

The clipping replicated on the following pages from a 1936 copy of the *Athol Daily News* lists trout streams and ponds of the Athol-Orange area then stocked by the state, before the Swift River watershed was flooded to create Quabbin. Some names listed in the article show common usage in 1936, although they are not used now. In the list of stocked waters in New Salem, for example, the name Tyre Brook is used, rather than Hop Brook now in familiar use. Pond fish distribution in New Salem refers to Hop Brook Pond, usually then called Moosehorn Pond. Under Petersham, both Sputtermill Brook and the west branch of Fever Brook are used, probably also referring to different sections of the same stream.

The article shows that the East Branch of Swift River below Pottapaug and the Middle Branch below the village of Soapstone were stocked with trout in 1936. Like the Millers River in Athol and Royalston, both those stretches of stream, now under the reservoir, provided primarily springtime fishing. The water was too warm in midsummer, with the exception of spring-fed areas, to support an active population of trout.

Incidentally, the second paragraph of the reprinted article is in error: the brooks listed were stocked with trout, and the ponds and lakes were stocked with pond fish, contrary to the statement.

LOCAL PONDS, BROOKS
STOCKED   WITH   FISH

Distribution Listed
For Anglers

(Special to the Daily News)
STATE HOUSE, Boston, April 4
That two local ponds and rivers have been stocked with pond fish and that six local streams and ponds have been stocked with trout, has been announced by the division of fisheries and game, in preparation for the 1936 fishing season.

Locally the division stocked the following with pond fish: West brook, Elmwood brook, Mill brook (upper end), Millers river Buckman brook and Newton brook, and trout were placed in the following waters White pond, Silver Lake and Lake Ellis.

In Worcester and Franklin counties, the following nearby streams have been stocked by the state to provide a paradise for modern Isaac Waltons'.

Athol; West brook, Elmwood brook, Mill brook, upper end, Millers river Bearsden bridge and above dam Union Twist Drill company, Buckman brook, and Newton brook.

Orange; Tully river, west brook; New Salem, Tyre brook, Moose Horn brook, Swift river, middle branch.

Dana; Fever brook, east and west branches, Swift river, east branch below Pottapaug, Swift river middle branch below Soapstone.

(continued)

Local Ponds

(Continued from Page 1)

Warwick; Warwick brook, Moss brook, Erving state forest, Tully brook, Mountain brook, Mount Grace state forest, and Gale brook.

Petersham; Stone brook, Swift river, east branch above Nichewaug, east branch at Harvard forest, east branch below Moulton's pond; Sputter mill brook; Fever brook, east branch and west branch; Moccasin brook; upper end above and below Williamsville road; Popple Camp brook.

Phillipston; Beaver brook, Popple Camp brook, Shattuck brook. Wendell; Lyons brook, Wendell state forest, Whetstone brook, Wendell state forest; Ruggles pond, Wendell state forest; Osgood brook.

Erving; Millers river, Laurel lake, Erving state forest, Keyup brook. Gill; Falls river and Otter Pond brook.

Royalston; Lawrence brook between South Royalston and Doans falls, between Perry Mill and Newton Mill, and above Perry's mill; Greeley brook, Len Moore brook, Sibley brook, Millers river below dam at toy factory, South Royalston, Collar brook, Priest brook, Otter River state forest.

Pond fish have been distributed in:

Athol: White pond, Silver lake, Lake Ellis.

Dana: Nesseponsett pond, Pottapaug pond.

Phillipston: Queen lake.

Royalston: Horseshoe (Church) pond, Long pond.

Erving: Long pond (Laurel lake), Connecticut river.

High water, Pelham, Massachusetts

Puppeyville, South New Salem, Massachusetts

Lower falls, Purgee Brook

Before Flooding of Quabbin

Pictures on these pages, generously provided from the collection of J. R. Greene, show sites in the Valley before it was flooded to create the Quabbin Reservoir. Bill Foye remembers fishing many of these places now under water. Some of the pictures are from photographic postcards.

"Pautaupaug Lake" (Pottapaug Pond), Dana, Massachusetts

Swift River Bridge, Dana, Massachusetts

Rattlesnake Ledges,
overlooking the West
Branch valley

Millpond, Millington, Massachusetts